MOVING FORWARD IN MID-CAREER

MOVING FORWARD IN MID-CAREER

A GUIDE TO REBUILDING YOUR CAREER AFTER BEING FIRED OR LAID OFF

JOHN HENRY WEISS

Skyhorse Publishing

Skyhorse Publishing books may be purchased in bulk at special discounts for sales promotion, corporate gifts, fund-raising, or educational purposes. Special editions can also be created to specifications. For details, contact the Special Sales Department, Skyhorse Publishing, 307 West 36th Street, 11th Floor, New York, NY 10018 or info@skyhorsepublishing.com.

Skyhorse® and Skyhorse Publishing® are registered trademarks of Skyhorse Publishing, Inc.®, a Delaware corporation.

Visit our website at www.skyhorsepublishing.com.

10 9 8 7 6 5 4 3 2 1

Library of Congress Cataloging-in-Publication Data is available on file.

Cover design by Rain Saukas

Print ISBN: 978-1-5107-5562-8
Ebook ISBN: 978-1-5107-2202-6

Printed in the United States of America

To Alice, Laura, Jane, and Chris, workers all, who have made their marks in the world of work.

CONTENTS

INTRODUCTION

Being fired or laid off is one of the most devastating events one can experience. For trauma, it ranks up there with divorce, loss of a loved one, and permanent personal injury. It is no longer that which happens to someone else. Most likely it will happen to you, too, when you least expect it . . . like in mid-career when you thought your job would last forever. Today, it is no longer thirty years with one company, a retirement dinner, a goldplated Apple Watch, and a fat pension.

It goes by different names: fired, bounced, riffed, sacked, whacked, downsized, canned, rightsized, laid off, let go, or whatever it might be called tomorrow. Regardless of what the process is called, the result is the same: you are no longer employed, which means that going forward you will have no paycheck, no bonus, and no benefits. And the title *Director of Marketing for Microsoft* will be gone too. Henceforward, you are just plain *Mary Jones*. When an employer decides that you are expendable, you are going, regardless of social status or length of time with the company. Not fair? Sorry. That's just the way it works.

The most serious error one can make after starting a new job, whether it is an entry-level position or a presidency, is to assume the job will last throughout the work cycle. In reality, how long will the job last? It could be six days, six weeks, six months, or six years. In today's workplace, all workers must prepare for the day when their jobs might end. For example, if you had been working with Ford in May 2017, you would have been facing a layoff because Ford had missed its quarterly revenue goal and subsequently announced that it was planning to cut 10 percent of its global workforce.

Many workers believe their jobs are secure and will last forever because of social status. They might think, "I'm a veteran. My employer won't let *me* go." Or *"I'm* a woman, and if they fire me, that's gender discrimination." Or "I'm sixty years old and they will never fire me and risk an age discrimination lawsuit." Or *"I'm* African American, and if they lay me off, that's racial discrimination." Dream on! This is not your grandparents' generation. Anyone is subject to being sacked on any given day for any reason.

How does it happen? Assume you have been on the payroll for two years. One ordinary workday, your boss calls you in for a chat. In the past, she has given you high fives for performance, but now she says your job has been eliminated because your division is not profitable. She has been ordered to reduce her staff by 50 percent. The company gives you a severance check and a folder of benefits, and you are escorted from the building by a security guard. You return home, seeking answers and wondering how you are going to survive.

Adding to the concern of losing a paycheck and benefits is the psychological trauma that accompanies being fired or laid off. Now you are just another human being trying to make it in a seemingly unfair world. Your thoughts and feelings run wild. You feel humiliated. You are angry. You blame everyone but yourself. You enter a period of deep grieving and possibly serious depression. You feel pressure to get a job, sometimes *any job*, to relieve the pain.

Losing your job will crush your ego like no other event because in our culture self-esteem and a positive self-image are closely tied to a job title and a company name. Working through the aftereffects of job loss and rebuilding a career is a serious matter. It involves more than crafting a dynamite resume and sending it off to numerous job boards and career pages. It's a process with many moving parts.

Job loss will negatively affect any worker regardless of rank, title, age, or time on task. However, mid-career workers suffer the most because they have the most to lose. They have high personal expenses like mortgage payments, car payments, various insurance premiums, student loans, and childcare. For them, losing a job has life-changing ramifications.

How does one cope with the trauma and begin the rebuilding process? How does one redefine persona? How does a discharged worker tread through the grieving process? Most importantly, how does one find new employment opportunities to make the bottom line black again? After we cut through the hype about fulfillment, purpose, and mission, this thing called *work* has a universal purpose—to make money in order to survive. No salary? No food, no shelter, no clothing. The bottom line is this: *work is all about the paycheck*, as crass as that might sound. Mission, fulfillment, and purpose are important but secondary.

Based on my experience in the staffing industry and on research from various sources, I have identified the major issues resulting from job loss. They are the basis for the six major themes that run through *Moving Forward*:

1. Losing a job is a major life crisis. Frequently, it comes unexpectedly, catching one unprepared to deal with its trauma and ramifications. Coping and rebuilding involve working through humiliation, denial, anger, blame, and grief, and finally accepting responsibility for your life and career going forward.

2. The majority of workers will have a series of jobs over the course of their working life. The era of "thirty years with AT&T, a retirement party, and a new smartphone" is over. On average, workers will change jobs six times during their working years.

3. Workers are fired or laid off for a variety of reasons, most of which are not related to their personal work productivity.

4. Fired workers must learn to fine-tune character and redefine persona independently of company affiliation or job title.

5. Searching for new career opportunities is productive only after recovering from the initial trauma of losing a job and after redefining career and life goals.

6. Secular and spiritual help can be instrumental in recovering and moving forward.

Moving Forward will guide your search for meaning and understanding while providing solutions for the challenges at each stage of the process, from the initial shock and humiliation of being let go to rebuilding your persona, examining your character, crafting a new resume, and seeking new employment opportunities. The book has two major objectives:

- To provide timely support for workers who have lost their jobs and are in process of rebuilding their careers.
- To provide job-hunting rubrics for workers reentering the job market.

The writing style of *Moving Forward* is informal, encouraging, conversational, and instructive. Each chapter concludes with two important features:

1. **Chapter Takeaways,** a series of succinct rubrics in bullet-point format.
2. **Print and Digital Resources,** a list of books and Internet references that extend the chapter content.

Throughout the book are personal stories of fired or laid-off workers that detail how they managed their job loss and what they did to move forward. They reflect a broad spectrum of the workplace: editors, sales representatives, marketing directors, presidents, video producers, and information technology managers.

You can read *Moving Forward* sequentially or proceed directly to chapters that have immediate appeal. Either way, the contents of this book will help you through the trauma, lead to a better understanding of who you really are, and help you through the process of building a new career.

So why did I decide to write this book? For two reasons.

1. In my job as an executive recruiter I witness firsthand the trauma that workers experience when let go in mid-career. This book is my solution to guide them through their crises and help them move forward into other careers.

2. I was laid off in mid-career myself, so I know from personal experience the many ramifications of this life event. When I was laid off, I had a huge home mortgage, car payments, insurance payments and tuition expenses for three children in college. I was laid off in a company-wide conference call with the CEO. I was given two days' notice, three weeks' severance pay, and two weeks of outplacement services. All other company employees suffered the same fate. Laid off in a conference call in mid-career? Does that really happen? Yes, it does, but I never thought something like that could happen to me. After my outplacement time, I vowed never again to work for someone else and started my own entrepreneurial business as an executive recruiter focusing on the education industry. That was twenty years ago and I have never looked back.

Part I

COPING WITH THE RAMIFICATIONS OF JOB LOSS

It takes 20 years to build a reputation and five minutes to ruin it. If you think about that, you'll do things differently.
—Warren Buffett

Chapter 1

HOW AND WHY WORKERS ARE FIRED OR LAID OFF

A typical day goes something like this for most workers. Wake up at six. Breakfast at seven. Report to work at eight. Do your thing until noon, with a break for coffee at ten. Lunch at twelve. Return to work at one and slug it out through the rest of the afternoon. Leave work at five and return home. Alternatively, on some days you might go shopping or for a drink with friends. Dinner at six. Then spend some quality time with the children, watch TV, or read a book. Maybe go to a movie with your spouse or partner. Go to bed between ten and eleven. This routine continues indefinitely until *something else* happens at work, usually late in the afternoon, near quitting time.

HOW THE LAYOFF PROCESS WORKS

That *something else* emerges like this. At 3:00 p.m. your boss invites you to the office of the human resources director for a chat. *A bit unusual but nothing to worry about*, you think. You know the HR director; nice woman, understanding, supportive. They call her Mrs. Friendly. Nothing to worry about. Probably some change in office routine or maybe a new office. Maybe an out-of-sequence performance evaluation. Maybe a promotion. Maybe a change in health benefits. She is all smiles and so is your boss who closes the door. Mrs. Friendly asks you to sit down in the chair in front of her desk. Your boss sits down beside you. Here's what happens next.

Your boss begins the chat saying something like this. "Joe, you have really made a solid contribution to the company, and we appreciate it. You were great. Always on time. Job requirements fulfilled. Good leadership potential. Nice job, Joe!" So far, so good. But why are your palms feeling a bit clammy? And what did the boss mean by "*were* great"?

Mrs. Friendly says, "Yes, Joe. I echo all of what your boss said. And I do like your last performance review. Nice job, and we thank you." *Hey*, you think. *How nice of them to single me out for some well-deserved recognition after three years on the job.*

She continues, "Joe, don't take personally what I'm going to say next because it has nothing to do with you. And I really mean that. However, the CEO and the president believe the company needs to cut expenses as we head into the next quarter. Unfortunately, the highest company expense is employee compensation. In order to save money and maintain profitability, we are having a reduction in force. So, Joe, we have to make some cuts, and it really pains me to tell you that we have decided to eliminate your position." Your boss nods his head in agreement. "And so, today is your last day working here, Joe. I'm truly sorry."

Then Mrs. Friendly hands you an envelope and says, "Joe, enclosed are your severance benefits which include your COBRA options, a check for your two remaining paid holidays for this year, and a check for three weeks of base salary, one week for each of the three years you worked with us. I know you will be happy with that. Your wife will be, too."

Now your boss chimes in: "Joe. I could not be more upset to see you go, but it happens sometimes. I'll give you a good recommendation. You will probably find something else very soon. Look, it's only 3:30, but you can leave early today. I'll walk you back to your office and wait while you collect your personal belongings and then escort you out of the building. Oh, by the way, we have already eliminated your company email address and shut down your company cell phone. And Ed, the security officer, will walk us to your car. Nothing personal. Just company procedure. Routine, Joe."

You don't know what to say to your boss or Mrs. Friendly. You are shocked into silence. In addition, you are humiliated because you feel the eyes of your coworkers sneaking peeks at you from their cubicles. You collect your personal items, including pictures of your wife and fifteen-month-old daughter, and walk out of the building in a daze, accompanied by the security officer and your former boss. You are hurt . . . hurt so much that your hands are trembling and you are mad as hell and humiliated in the extreme.

And you wonder out loud, "Why didn't my colleague, Marsha, get sacked like I did? And what about Bill? He's still there. All of us had comparable jobs in the marketing department. What am I going to tell my wife? I didn't do anything wrong, so why did they let me go? Was I fired? Laid off? What's going on here? Maybe I should get an attorney to sort this out."

Does it really happen like that? Count on it. On any given day, thousands of workers will be fired just as you were. Use any euphemism you want, but when your employer tells you to leave the premises, consider yourself fired. However, you can use *laid off* or *let go* if it makes you feel better.

So what's next, Mr. Fired? First, it means finding another job in order to put food on the table for you, your wife, and your kid. And a roof over your head for you, your wife, and your kid. And clothing for you, your wife, and your kid. In addition, it means collecting your unemployment compensation check each month, with embarrassment. By God, you never imagined that you would be on welfare! A college degree was supposed to prevent this from occurring. Now what, food stamps? Section 8 housing? A government cell phone? Medicaid? Asking friends and family for a long-term, no-interest loan?

The first next step means finding another job—any job, you believe, to stop the nightmare. This means going through the job-hunting process again, a hated activity that keeps you awake nights. Resumes? Interviews? Rejection? Who needs it! You get advice from everyone: your spouse, your friends, your industry network, your neighbors, and those irritating bloggers who tell you that finding another job is just a matter of crafting a *dynamite resume*, which they will do for a price. And so you sit at your computer day in and day out scouring the job boards and firing off your brilliant resume to places like Box 21, Position 47, and Employment Manager. The result? Nothing. Might as well send your brilliant piece of dynamite to the third ring of the planet Saturn.

Finding new employment is not just a matter of creating a resume and firing it off to multiple job boards. It is a multistep process that requires your patience, time, and understanding.

WHAT TO DO AND NOT TO DO AFTER LOSING YOUR JOB

In a *US News and World Report* article, Alison Green lists ten things to do immediately after being let go. They are:

- Don't panic.
- Don't freak out.
- Don't do anything rash.
- Don't sign a severance agreement immediately.
- Negotiate how your departure will be described.
- Look over your finances.
- File for unemployment.
- Plan to keep in touch with clients and coworkers.
- Remain objective.
- Remember that you're not alone.

This list is a good starting point to rebuilding your career. Consider it a bit of first aid to get past the initial trauma. The last bullet point is something to always keep in mind as you navigate the rest of your working years. Today, as you are reading this page, thousands of workers will get laid off just as you did . . . through no fault of their own. Being laid off, being fired, and being hired are just impersonal events in the world of business. (This brings to mind my experience, being laid off in a company-wide conference call. Laid off by phone? It does not get more impersonal than that.)

We hear so much from the pundits, financial gurus, and national media about companies letting go thousands of workers at a crack. One might think that the US economy is in a constant state of recession. Reality, however, is much different. Workers are let go for a number of reasons, all of which have to do with the numbers. A look at the reasons why workers are laid off will set the record straight.

WHY MID-CAREER WORKERS LOSE THEIR JOBS. IT'S ALL ABOUT THE NUMBERS

Learning *why* workers are laid off is important not only for those out of work now, but also for those still working because one never knows when the ax will fall. Going forward, you will be looking for *good* job opportunities, not just *any* job. This requires information about how employers operate, why they do what they do—like lay off ten thousand workers at a crack. The last thing you need is to jump into another job that will disappear in six months. To avoid that potential tragedy, you need to do your homework while you are unemployed, or still employed and preparing for what could happen on any work day at 3:30 pm.

One could argue night and day about why workers are laid off or fired. You hear one story from the academics, another from business executives, another from the talking heads on the financial channels, and still another from politicians. And do not forget the chatter on social media. To cut through the hype, let's go to the numbers.

Workers are constantly being downsized, reorganized, or right-sized. For example, data from the Bureau of Labor Statistics indicates that approximately 55,000 workers are fired or laid off each day. *That's approximately 20 million per year!* On the plus side, millions of workers will be hired each day. Because of this constant churning in the workplace, workers will change jobs an average of six times during their working years.

The American workplace employs over 155 million workers, making *our workforce alone* the world's eighth largest "country." There are many moving parts in the workplace, some working in sync and others fighting against each other. Employers are constantly revising plans, merging, acquiring competitors, moving operations to another country, going into bankruptcy, and going out of business. All of this means that workers are going to lose their jobs. For you, the laid-off worker, it is important to remember that being let go is usually *not about you personally*. It's about an employer fighting to survive and remain profitable.

THE UNEMPLOYMENT RATE

Daily, we hear the pundits, talking heads, and media gurus screaming about one of their favorite topics—the unemployment rate. To
hear them talk, one would think that America is heading for financial disaster with unemployment taking a leading role. The numbers
help us sort fact from fiction. And they will help you understand why
you got that sorrowful "goodbye, Joe" from the human resources
director at 3:30 p.m. on a day you were not expecting it.

The average rate of unemployment in the United States since the
Great Depression has been approximately 6 percent. Many econo-
mists interpret that to mean that an employment rate of 94 percent is
truly full employment. Since 1970, our lowest rate of unemployment
was 3.8 percent in 2019, and the highest was 10 percent in 2009.

The three main causes for unemployment are *seasonal* unemployment, when workers are laid off because of bad weather; *structural*
unemployment, when workers are laid off because their jobs are replaced by technology; and *cyclical* unemployment, when workers are
laid off because of changes in the economy, such as a recession that
weakens consumer demand for products and services. These three
causes of unemployment will always be present. There will never be
such a thing as 0 percent unemployment.

The numbers tell us that America has an average *employment*
rate of 94 percent. If workers in America claim they can't find work,
it is not the fault of the president, elected officials, their teachers, or
their mothers and fathers. The fault lies with them alone. If you really want a job, it is there for the taking—if you use the rules for job
hunting in this book and other resources.

FACTORS THAT CONTRIBUTE TO JOB LOSS

Six major factors are responsible for the large number of job losses
each year.

1. ***Reduction in force.*** Businesses exist to make money. If they
   make money, they remain in business and grow, which results
   in more hiring. This applies to *for-profit* and *nonprofit*
   businesses alike. If a company does not make money after

deducting expenses and taxes, it will go out of business and workers will lose their jobs. To maintain profitability companies are constantly adjusting the size of their staff. For example, when a fast food company like McDonald's experiences a downturn in profits over a period of two or more quarters, it will downsize its staff. The result? Massive layoffs. This process is frequently called a reduction in force, a *RIF*. Those laid off in this process are referred to as having been *riffed*.

2. *Mergers.* Tens of thousands of companies combine forces each year for a variety of reasons. When two companies merge their operations, workers are laid off. For example, when company A and company B merge, the new company C will need only one vice president of sales. The result? One of the VPs from A or B will be laid off.

3. *Acquisitions.* You hear it every day. "Company X buys company Y." Again, when two companies are combined into one, workers are laid off to prevent duplication of services. Also, businesses sometimes sell only their products or services. The result? Massive layoffs occur because the acquiring company does not take the employees, only the products. It is called an asset acquisition.

4. *Trade deals that send jobs overseas.* Staff employees are usually the last to hear that their American employer cut a deal to have their products manufactured in a foreign country. It is only after the layoffs that workers learn their jobs were lost because the company's products can be made more cheaply outside of the United States. The same applies to services. For example, when was the last time you spoke to an American-based customer service worker? And what is the country of origin of your new pair of Nike shoes?

5. *Bankruptcies.* When a company is consistently unprofitable, it uses the business tactic called bankruptcy to pay off creditors. When a company files for bankruptcy, what usually follows is a reorganization, which results in massive layoffs.

6. *Reorganizations.* Periodically, companies reorganize to improve day-to-day operations. For example, General Electric moved its corporate home office from Connecticut to Massachusetts. GE offered to relocate workers with key positions, but this was not acceptable for those firmly rooted in Connecticut. Those who did not accept that offer were laid off along with workers in support positions. The same thing happened to workers employed by Merck in some of its New Jersey offices. When the company decided to relocate some operations to other states, many workers were laid off. Frequently, it is less costly for companies to lay off workers and hire new talent in the new location.

When you are seeking a new job, it is prudent to learn as much as you can about a potential employer's plans going forward. This information is available from company press releases, from TV interviews with company executives, and from company hiring managers during interviews for a new position.

MOVING FORWARD

Being fired or laid off is a traumatic experience, one like no other for a mid-career worker with financial and family responsibilities. All workers who have been let go, regardless of the reason, experience several stages of grieving, and it is of paramount importance to deal with this process as soon as possible. In the next chapter, we will identify the various stages of grieving and provide help for moving through them as quickly as possible.

CHAPTER TAKEAWAYS
- Working for someone else is a hazardous occupation.
- No job is forever. Always remain is a state of readiness to look for another job.
- Companies lay off workers primarily for business reasons, not personal reasons.

PRINT AND DIGITAL RESOURCES

Berman, Karen, and Joe Knight. *Financial Intelligence: A Manager's Guide to Knowing What the Numbers Really Mean.* Harvard Business Review Press, 2013.

Doyle, Alison. "The Difference Between Getting Fired and Getting Laid Off." *The Balance,* December 6, 2016. https://www.thebalance.com/difference-between-getting-fired-and-getting-laid-off-2060743.

Molly's Middle America. www.mollysmiddleamerica.blogspot.com.

US Small Business Administration, SBA, www.sba.gov.

US Department of Commerce, www.commerce.gov.

Chapter 2

WORKING THROUGH THE GRIEVING PROCESS

When I was laid off in mid-career, I thought that finding another job would be a quick and easy process. After all, I had been in the educational technology business for quite some time working with the likes of Apple Computer. Write a resume, make some phone calls, and a job will follow, fast. However, I was caught off guard when I entered the grieving process after losing my job because of an asset acquisition. Everyone goes through a period of grieving after a significant loss, which could be the death of a loved one, loss of a spouse by divorce, loss of a physical function through permanent injury, *or loss of a job*. Losing a job frequently triggers a period of grieving as severe as that caused by death or divorce. For verification, ask anyone who has been let go.

The severity of the grieving process caused by job loss is proportionate to the separated worker's rank, compensation, and age. Mid-career workers usually suffer the most because they have the most to lose in terms of status, rank, and compensation. They are likely to have significant mortgage or rental payments, automobile payments, credit card payments, childcare expenses, college tuition payments, insurances payments, and more. Being forced to deal with all of those responsibilities will throw most laid-off workers into the classical stages of the grieving process.

CLASSICAL STAGES OF THE GRIEVING PROCESS

Swiss-born psychiatrist Elisabeth Kübler-Ross worked with termi-nally ill patients and their loved ones and noted certain patterns that emerged in the dying process. In her book *On Death and Dying*, she states that there are five stages in the grieving process:

1. Denial
2. Anger
3. Bargaining
4. Depression
5. Acceptance

The length of time one stays in the grieving process is propor-tional to the closeness of the bond between the two individuals. The closer the bond, the longer it takes to move ahead and restore normal life balance. Most people work through the grieving process using their own resources, but others require professional help from a psy-chologist, psychiatrist, clergy member, or career counselor.

THE GRIEVING PROCESS EXPERIENCED BY LET-GO WORKERS

In my work as an executive recruiter, I have seen laid-off workers go through a grieving process parallel to that experienced by death of a loved one. However, it is usually abbreviated because work-ers quickly become preoccupied with finding another job, a time-consuming task that pushes the worker through the grieving process. I have noted the following stages of grief when counseling, and con-soling, job candidates who have lost their jobs, especially those in mid-career.

Denial

After hearing those torturous words from the boss or the human re-sources director, "We have to let you go," most workers say aloud or silently, "This can't be happening to me. I've given my blood, sweat, and tears to this company and there is no reason why I should be laid off." Many workers refuse to believe they were asked to leave the premises and petition the boss and HR director for reinstatement.

If that does not work, they persist in seeking reasons for dismissal that make sense to them. They want more than "We're having a reorganization." Some take it to the next level and demand to see their boss's boss or the president or CEO. Usually, the appeal to a higher authority bears no fruit and the laid-off worker leaves the premises dejected but still in denial.

After leaving the premises, some workers take it to the next step, seeking help from a colleague in the company. Some ask a company friend to intercede with the boss or human resources director to reinstate their jobs. Others seek the help of a lawyer to have their employment reinstated. These initiatives are rarely successful.

Humiliation

A person who has just been told that their presence in the company is no longer needed feels a great sense of humiliation. When it happens, it seems that the eyes of all coworkers are on you. You feel that *they* know that you were sacked. Word travels fast. The most humiliating event is being walked out of the workplace accompanied by a security officer as though you committed a crime. It hurts like nothing else and sets you up for the next stage, anger.

Anger

A worker enters the anger stage of the grieving process when attempts to become reinstated have failed, and when the humiliation continues as more people become aware that you were let go. Anger is usually directed at three sources: the company, the boss, and the human resources director, the one who frequently delivers the bad news. If not resolved quickly, the anger stage will prevent the fired worker from thinking clearly and planning the next step, rebuilding their career. Usually, workers in the anger stage will hurl epithets at the boss and the company to anyone who will listen. Some will curse using language heretofore unused. Some will lose it completely and resort to violence by physically injuring the human resources director or the boss. When you find yourself in a prolonged stage of anger, do everything possible to move forward, like seeking counseling from a psychologist, a career coach, or a clergy member.

Depression

Fired or laid-off workers lose that sense of professional identity that sets them apart from the rest of the pack. Frequently, laid-off workers enter a stage of pessimism, inadequacy, helplessness, and despondency, which is manifested by constant complaining to family members, friends, colleagues, and anyone who will listen to their tale of woe. Unfortunately, for some workers it goes beyond constant complaining, and they enter a state of depression that requires clinical help from a psychiatrist. However, most work through this stage of the grieving process by activating their network of family and friends for support and encouragement.

Acceptance

Acceptance is the final stage of the grieving process for those who have lost their jobs. In previous stages of the process you may have tried to resolve the problem but to no avail. You are not going to be rehired. Period. You must put the past behind you and move forward, but on your own terms. Acceptance is a liberating process. It closes the grieving stage and enables you to move forward to rebuild not only your career, but also your entire life. In a sense, being fired or laid off can prove to be one of the best things that has ever happened to you. When you accept your situation, you take total ownership not only of your career, but also of your entire life.

> Put aside your regrets of the past.
> Put away your fear of the future.
> Move forward with confidence.

FIVE SOLUTIONS FOR WORKING THROUGH THE GRIEVING PROCESS

Workers at every rank can move through the grieving process using these resources: the Internet, print and digital books and magazines, a career coach, a friend or family member, faith-based resources, an outplacement service, and common sense. I have witnessed let-go workers use some or all of these resources to move forward successfully. Here are five initiatives to hasten your trip through the grieving process.

Take a Break

The first thing most let-go workers do is plunge into the job-hunting process, and that is a huge mistake. First, take a well-deserved break. Consider beginning the process by going out to an upscale restaurant or pub today or tomorrow, preferably with a trusted friend. Go out and let loose. Have a good time. Lift your glass and get it off your chest shouting the title of a song made famous by country singer Johnny Paycheck, "Take This Job and Shove It!" Pay in cash and leave a generous tip. While you are at dinner, begin planning the next step—leaving the house and having more fun.

The day following your night on the town, make a written list of activities for the next seven days that you can do alone. Do not include anything work related. You will have time for that later. Include in your list all of those things you could not do when you were working because your job sapped all of your time and energy. (Remember those irritating text messages at 10:00 p.m.?) Plan to leave the house each day to participate in physical activities such as visiting museums and art galleries, playing golf, swimming, hiking, skiing, biking, mountain climbing, and exploring locations that arouse your curiosity. Make sure they take place away from home. At the conclusion to this week of physical activity, move forward to the next step, leaving town.

If you have enough discretionary income, leave town for a week, preferably alone, to a faraway national or international destination. You can find attractive and reasonably priced travel deals with a bit of research. How would you like six days in Ireland? London? How about nine days touring the Grand Canyon, Sedona, Monument Valley, Bruce and Zion National Parks? Getting out of town is the best remedy I know to forget about the past, particularly about that nasty employer who had the temerity to let you go. The hell with them! Move on. You can live without them. Truth be known, you never really liked working there. Other jobs are out there, as you will discover upon returning home from your vacation.

Take a Personal Inventory

Make a list of all of the good things that you still have: your spouse or partner, children, family members, friends, intelligence, job skills, energy, and education. Your former employer could not take all of that away from you. Most of all, you still have your attitudes and opinions, which you will use moving forward. You are still intact.

In addition, record the personal possessions that your work has enabled you to acquire (i.e., the best of the basic three: food, shelter, clothing). While millions in the world will go to bed hungry tonight, you will not. Be thankful for what you have and remember that you are among the most fortunate people in the world, a worker in the United States. While millions of people from around the world are banging on the door of America in order to get a job, you are already here. As a mid-career worker, most likely you have reached an income level in your previous job that placed you in the upper 15 percent of the income bracket. Looking at the numbers always puts things in perspective.

Study the Numbers

When you are out of a job, there is a tendency to hear only the bad news. Tune out the media babble about the dire state of the economy and conduct your own research. Study the numbers from the Bureau of Labor Statistics, the Department of Commerce, and the Pew Research Center.

Also, look at the employment rate (as opposed to the unemployment rate) in America and others countries. As I discussed earlier, we have had an average employment rate of 94 percent over the past seventy years. Look at European countries, like Greece, where the employment rate is a mere 75 percent, and you will count your blessings. It does not get better than living in America when you are looking for a job. .

Evaluate Your Work-Life Balance

For some fortunate workers, work-life balance was never a problem. Their employers were cognizant of the fact that life existed away from the office, storefront, or construction site and planned the work day accordingly. However, for others, especially those whose jobs were technology driven, work never seemed to go away. Tweets at 10:00 p.m. on a Tuesday from the boss. Texts at 8:00 a.m. on a Saturday requesting a work-flow summary for a meeting on Monday morning. An email at 7:00 p.m. on Friday "asking" you to show up for an emergency meeting the next day. What did you usually do after work? Did your last job, where you worked sixty hours a week, leave you so exhausted that you can't recall when you last visited an art museum or seen a movie? Were there any "after work" hours, or were work and personal life one and the same?

Define your life priorities beginning with family responsibilities: spouse, children, parents. Next, write down what brings you pleasure and satisfaction in your life *outside of work* and after fulfilling family responsibilities. In your last job, how much time did you devote to those strictly personal pursuits? One hour each day? Maybe a few hours on the weekend after the usual household chores? Vow that you will never again permit an employer to control your life. This is *your* life. Define it on your own terms.

Evaluate Your Work History and Objectives

Did you really like your last job or did you go there every day solely for the money? Do you want to continue working in your specialty or would you be happy to move forward to something else? Many workers fall into a specific area in the workplace for which they really have no particular liking. It may have been the need to pay off the student loan after graduating with a master's and the most easily accessible job that had an above-average compensation level was one in sales, first as a territory sales rep, then as a district manager, and most recently as a regional sales manager. You were on the road more than 50 percent of the time, rushing from one airport and hotel to another. You were constantly making pipeline reports and evaluations of your subordinates. Did you really enjoy that? If not, define and write down your five ideal jobs. Are you ready to move to a new career? Will one of your five ideal jobs provide the compensation you need to maintain your desired style of living and meet current living expenses?

If your financial situation is such that you can make a change, do it now. Why wait until you are thinking about retirement?

MOVING FORWARD

Transitioning to the acceptance stage of the grieving process is a pre-requisite for moving forward to defining a new you, independent of job rank or title. However, it is important to evaluate your financial situation to make sure that you can meet obligations related to your own personal well-being and that of your family and your dependents. In succeeding chapters, we'll examine the financial ramifications of job loss and what you can do to minimize the impact. Stay tuned.

CHAPTER TAKEAWAYS

- All let-go workers experience a period of grieving.
- Accepting the fact that you were laid off and have no chance of having your job reinstated is a liberating experience.
- Put away the regrets of the past.
- Forget your fears of the future.
- Move forward to another career in America, the breadbasket of the world where jobs are always available for those who know how and where to find them.

PRINT AND DIGITAL RESOURCES

Froehls, Michael. *The Gift of Job Loss.* Peitho Publishing, 2011.

"Job Loss and Unemployment Stress." *HelpGuide.org.* www.helpguide.org/articles/stress/job-loss-and-unemployment-stress.htm.

Kyosaki, Robert. *Rich Dad. Poor Dad.* Plata Publishing LLC, 2012.

Warrell, Margie. "Bouncing Back from Job Loss: The 7 Habits of Highly Effective Job Hunters." *Forbes,* June 12, 2012. https://www.forbes.com/sites/womensmedia/2012/06/12/bouncing-back-from-job-loss-the-7-habits-of-highly-effective-job-hunters/#240b15147b70.

Willink, Jocko, and Leif Babin. *Extreme Ownership: How U.S. Navy Seals Lead and Win.* St. Martin's Press, 2015.

Chapter 3

PROTECTING AND MAINTAINING YOUR SAVINGS, INVESTMENTS, AND IRA

When the paycheck stops, there might be a knee-jerk reaction to begin liquidating savings and other assets in order to continue your lifestyle as though you were still on the payroll. Nothing could be riskier. Even though you are out of work and have no regular paycheck, it is important to evaluate, monitor, and preserve the financial gains you have made. Make this a priority.

Remember that your out-of-work situation is temporary. The paycheck will return when you move forward with another job. While redefining your persona and rebuilding your character, evaluate all of your assets and decide what you are going to do to preserve them.

PROTECTING ALL OF YOUR INVESTMENTS

An investment is anything that has monetary value: savings accounts, individual retirement accounts, non-IRA brokerage accounts, credit cards, mutual funds, real estate holdings, and personal possessions.

Financial investments should be monitored constantly because of the cyclical nature of our economy. The last thing you need is to see your investments lose significant value overnight. It happened in the Great Recession of 2008, and it can happen again. Remember that two consecutive quarters of negative gross domestic product (GDP) herald a recession, a time to move your money to a safe haven like cash, which can be reinvested when the economy emerges from the recession. (You can learn more about how to monitor the economy by tuning in to financial TV channels like CNBC, Fox Business, and Bloomberg Business.)

Protecting Your Cash Savings

Being let go usually comes when you are least expecting it. The first thing that the laid-off worker may think about is how much money they have in the bank to carry them through the period of unemployment. Is the cash you have in the bank enough to cover expenses until you have a new income stream? According to a study conducted by the Financial Industry Regulatory Authority (FINRA), 56 percent of US workers do not have enough in their cash accounts to cover three months of necessary expenses. Alarmingly, a new study reveals that seven out of ten American workers have less than $1,000 in their savings account. This borders on a national tragedy and reveals that the majority of adult workers have not learned the basics of money management. Every worker, regardless of income level, should keep enough money in a cash account to cover at least six months of expenses. My recommendation is to keep an extra margin for safety and make it twelve months at all times during your working years.

Establishing a Six-Month Emergency Fund
To determine where you stand financially after losing your job, make a list of all *necessary* monthly expenses. Do not include money that you would spend on items like going out to dinner, going to concerts, ball games or shows, purchasing the latest fashion items advertised on TV or social media, the latest clothing and digital apps for the children, new cell phones, new pets, and new furniture. Include on your list only those items that are absolutely necessary, such as mortgage payments, car payments, children's tuition, insurance premiums, utility bills, tax payments, food, and critical clothing needs for yourself and family members.

After determining your monthly expenses, multiply by six to learn what you will need to carry you through a six-month period of unemployment. If you do not have a sufficient amount in your money market or savings account to cover necessary expenses for six months, the average length of time it should take to find a new employment opportunity, establish an emergency fund. Do this by transferring money from other sources, like your personal investment portfolio.

Transfer only what you need to cover these expenses. For example, if you determine that your estimated six month expenses are $24,000 and you have just $15,000 in ready cash, transfer only $9,000 from your personal investments to cover costs. This might require selling favorite equities or mutual funds. In extreme situations, it may require withdrawing from your IRA, but remember that this carries a 10 percent IRS tax penalty if you are under the age of 59 ½.

Protect your newly created cash emergency fund by resisting the temptation to buy unnecessary items. When you find another job, rebuild your emergency fund to the $24,000 level, the amount of money required to pay for six months of expenses. Your newly created cash emergency account will build the confidence you need to make the right employment choices moving forward.

Protecting Your IRA

This is an opportune time to reevaluate your entire financial position. If you were enrolled in a company-sponsored IRA with your previous employer, you had a certain amount withdrawn from your paycheck and invested in an IRA mutual fund. Most workers believe the company and the fund looked after your best interests but . . . did they? Now is the time to evaluate the mutual funds in your IRA. What kind of funds are they? Bond funds? Equity funds? ETFs? Money market funds? Domestic funds? International funds? How much does the mutual fund company charge in annual fees? How much do they charge for making changes to your account? A 1 percent fee could add up to thousands of dollars over the life time of your IRA. You do not have to leave your IRA with the company used by your former employer. You can easily transfer the IRA to another company. The move is transparent and you lose nothing in the process. Usually the transfer can be completed by phone in a few minutes.

There are a number of reputable companies to consider for your IRA. Two of the most popular are Vanguard and Fidelity. They have very low administrative fees and buy/sell fees. Most of their funds do not have a front-end load, which is a fee assessed for buying into a specific mutual fund.

If you have dependent children, consider establishing a 529 College Savings Account, a plan that offers many advantages. Your IRA provider will help you either online or by phone to establish the 529.

Moving forward in the second half of your career, I recommend that you assume total control over your IRA rather than permitting your employer to make the decision for you. Evaluate all of your options and select those that best meet your objectives.

MONITORING COSTS OF THE BASICS

This in-between-jobs time is ideal to make an objective review of all your possessions. Begin by making a written inventory of everything you own. Place a value beside each item. Decide whether it is a short-term item that you can modify downward or live without.

Automobiles

Transportation-related expenses are likely to be included in your list of necessary items. However, it is advisable to examine your current situation to see if changes can be made to cut down the costs. If you live in the middle of the city, for instance in Chicago, New York, Boston, San Francisco, or Washington, DC, maybe a car is unnecessary because you can walk or take public transportation to and from work. If you want to leave town on weekends, you can always rent a car or use Uber. Choosing this option will save thousands of dollars in car cost, insurance, parking, and maintenance.

If you do need a car, evaluate the make and model of car you are driving. Did you ever consider why you need that particular car to get from point A to point B? Downsizing your car or moving to a hybrid model could result in savings totaling thousands of dollars.

Food

Like transportation, food is a necessary expense, but you can control its cost. Pay close attention to your food spending habits. Do you go to the supermarket and just load your basket with things you like regardless of cost? You can save a bundle by evaluating every item you pick up. For example, take the traditional box of corn flakes. Recently, I went to my local supermarket and purchased an eighteen-ounce box of corn flakes. I had two choices: the Kellogg brand at $4.17 or the store brand at $1.99. I selected the store brand and saved $2.18. Multiple savings like this over time, and you save thousands on food purchases. By the way, the store-brand corn flakes looked the same and tasted the same as the Kellogg brand.

Another stealth expense can be food purchased at restaurants. For example, the cost for a burger and fries is approximately $13. Add $3.00 for a beverage, $1.00 for tax, $3.00 for a tip, and you have chalked up $20.00. Do that five times a week and you spend $100; for a month, it's $400, a lot of money for a load of cholesterol. The same applies to eating upscale. Go to a medium-grade restaurant, and the average price for an entree is $22.00. Add a beverage at $8.00, a dessert at $8.00, tax at $1.80, and a $7.00 tip, and your total bill is $46.80. Do that four times a month and you spend $187.20. Over six months, the average length of time you could be out of work, your restaurant bill is $1,123.20. When you are out of work, you do not need to eat out every week. When you do, allot a certain amount of money for your meal before looking at the menu.

Shelter

Next, consider the item that has become a national obsession—housing. Why is it that we spend so much of our time and money on shelter? Why is it that we are constantly "moving up" the shelter chain to something larger and more luxurious? Do you really need a house or apartment of the size that you live in now?

Rethink your housing needs considering the risk of losing your job. It is possible, in fact probable, that you will face another layoff as the economy changes. I am not implying that you should downsize immediately after being laid off. It is just something to consider when rebuilding your career and lifestyle.

Clothing

The cost of clothing is huge. The next time you are dressed in business attire, add up the cost of everything on your person, from underwear to jewelry. For men, the cost will be at least $500. For women, it will be approximately the same if the cost of jewelry is added. If you have children, make a cost inventory for them as well.

Clothing is a stealth cost because we have gone online to purchase much of it. It is so easy to do. A skirt from Talbots. Shoes from Nordstrom. Nike shoes for the kids from Amazon. We charge these online purchases to credit cards. When you had a paycheck on a regular basis, you thought nothing of paying that bill online. In the entire process, you never touched money, paper or coin. When you spend money in the cloud, you lose track of value. Now, when you receive the bill at the end of the month, you are shocked at the total.

While unemployed, set a strict budget for clothing. Buy only what you need for yourself and family members. Go back to brick-and-mortar stores and pay for clothing using real money, not credit cards. The high cost of this basic necessity will once again become a reality and enable you to control your clothing costs.

Education

What can you do to cut expenses if you have children moving toward college when you have just been laid off? A year at a middle-ranked private college will cost at least $40,000 per year. An Ivy League university will set you back at least $60,000 per year. Even your state college will cost $20,000 or more per year. Why send your kids off to a high-priced college now when they do not have the slightest clue about what they would like to do with the rest of their lives? While you can't tell your children to stop their education while you are unemployed, you can be creative and consider these short-term alternatives that will work to their benefit and save money for the family:

- Have your child take a year off after high school, a gap year as it is called, and work to learn what this world is all about. After that, send your child genius to a community college for two years to learn what a college education means short and long term. It may be that your child/student will discover that a hands-on job like carpentry or photography is more in line with their interests and aptitude.
- Another alternative is studying for an online degree while working part time. We are slowly learning that the traditional four years of bricks-and-mortar college immediately following high school makes little sense for many of our teenagers.

MOVING FORWARD

The most important thing you can do while out of work and out of a paycheck is to protect your finances. But what happens after you cut to the bone and still need money to carry on? How do you replace the income you lost? There are common-sense ways to survive this temporary monetary crisis. I'll tell you what to do and how to do it in the next chapter, "Replacing Income."

CHAPTER TAKEAWAYS

- Always keep six months of expense money in cash reserves.
- Constantly monitor your expenses and financial assets.
- Take total control of your IRA.
- Your possessions are investments. Evaluate their usefulness and cut back if they are expendable.
- Once you have found a new job, prepare for the next crisis, which may be losing your job again.

PRINT AND DIGITAL RESOURCES

Bloomberg Business News TV, 6:00 a.m.–10:00 p.m.
Bureau of Labor Statistics, www.bls.gov.
CNBC Financial News, CNBC TV. 6:00 a.m.–7:00 p.m.
Fox Business News, Fox Business Channel. 6:00 a.m.–8:00 p.m.
Mad Money with Jim Cramer, CNBC TV, 6:00 p.m.

Chapter 4

REPLACING INCOME

Replacing the paycheck after losing a job is an immediate and serious challenge for all workers. There are few events more jarring than losing your source of income, which we need not only to supply the basics needed now, but also for future security. Every worker grapples with this issue regardless of income level. When the paycheck stops, the fun ends as well. Here are some viable options to deal with this mess.

TAPPING INTO FIVE SOURCES OF INCOME WHILE UNEMPLOYED

Usually, employers provide let-go workers with severance packages, which vary in form and content from one company to another. To make sure you are receiving what is owed to you by the company, check the offer letter you received when you joined the company. It is common for companies to award one week of severance pay for each year worked to those in mid-level management positions. Workers at the director level and up will receive greater severance pay.

The severance package is an important benefit. Use it wisely while you continue through the process of rebuilding your career. It is akin to receiving a paid vacation. Use this period of respite to plan your strategies for replacing income while you are unemployed. Here are five ways to ensure that you will have sufficient financial resources during your period of unemployment.

Immediately Apply for Unemployment Compensation

Some call it the safety net system. Others call it welfare. Whatever the term, it is the best system we have to help unemployed workers through a difficult time. It is referred to as unemployment compensation, unemployment benefits, or unemployment insurance depending upon the jurisdiction and the type of separation from the employer. The system originated in 1935 when President Franklin Delano Roosevelt signed into law the Social Security Act. It has had many iterations over the years. Always check to see what is owed to you.

Do not confuse workers' compensation with unemployment compensation. They are two different programs. Workers' compensation provides benefits for workers who suffer injuries while on the job. Unemployment compensation provides benefits for workers who are laid off.

Unemployment compensation comes from the joint federal and state operation that was devised to provide substitute income for workers who lost their jobs. It is administered by each individual state. There are well-defined requirements that must be met in order to collect these benefits. The employer who terminated you must disclose your unemployment benefits before you leave the premises. If this did not happen, immediately contact the human resources director of your former employer for an explanation of how the benefits apply in your situation and what the procedures are to apply for benefits. In addition, contact your local unemployment office for advice and guidance. You can do that by phone, but the best way to get immediate results is to make a personal call at the nearest office.

Some workers are hesitant to tap into the system because of embarrassment, arrogance, or fear of hurtful gossip. However, remember that the system was created to help unemployed workers provide for the basics for a limited period of time and is funded in great part by unemployment insurance paid for by the employer and the worker through payroll tax deductions. You have paid for this insurance. Use its benefits whether your income was $5,000 per month or $20,000 per month.

Stereotypes abound depicting the "type" of person collecting unemployment benefits. They are frequently thought of as uneducated and holding low-skill jobs. Think again. I learned firsthand about people collecting unemployment compensation when I was laid off after the company I was working for was sold. I had a mortgage payment, a car payment, insurance payments, and college tuition bills for three of my children. Soon after being laid off in a companywide conference call, I visited my local unemployment insurance office. It was a bare-bones environment crowded with hundreds of unemployed workers applying for benefits. Some were dressed in upscale office attire, some in casual clothing, and others in clothing worn for hands-on jobs. While waiting my turn to meet with a counselor, I spoke with a physician, a sales rep, and a truck driver, all unemployed, like me. All of us were in the same boat—let go and needing a short-term fix to survive. It was a humbling experience, and from it I learned something that you could not find in a textbook or an Internet search. My benefits lasted for three months. I used this time to explore my career path and decided to start my own business, executive recruiting in the for-profit education industry. Without the unemployment benefits to carry me through a very challenging period of my life, my future may have taken an unwanted direction.

Seek Part-Time Work with Your Previous Employer

Occasionally, the employer who let you go will hire you back to undertake a specific task on a contract basis. Why? Because it saves the employer money. This arrangement has benefits for both you and the employer. For you, it keeps the paycheck coming in, and for the employer it eliminates the added cost of benefits, usually about 30 percent of base salary. To make this happen, you must take the initiative and make a proposal to the employer. For example, employers who exhibit at trade shows need company-knowledgeable workers to administer the operation with the convention centers, display companies, and transportation companies such as FedEx, in addition to coordinating schedules of company employees who will staff the exhibit booths. Sometimes the company has one of the marketing staff handle these tasks, but when workers are let go, the job of coordinating trade shows is outsourced to reduce costs. Who better than a laid-off employee who knows the company's products and operations to coordinate trade shows on a part-time basis? To initiate the process, contact your former HR director or marketing director and present them with a proposal to manage trade shows on a per-event basis. An added benefit is that you will meet numerous potential employers at the convention center hosting the event you coordinated.

Seek Part-Time Work with a New Employer

While you are looking for new employment opportunities, you have the option of seeking a part-time job with an entirely new employer, maybe in an entirely new business. Job hunting can be a full-time activity, but you can allocate a certain number of hours to working on weekends. Remaining active in the workplace will build your network, enable you to explore alternate job opportunities, and keep you mentally alert.

Make Reallocations to Your Personal Investment Portfolio

If you need serious extra money and have a personal portfolio of investments in equities, consider selling some or all of them and using the money to purchase income-producing bonds. Use the monthly dividends as income. You can purchase individual bonds or buy into a bond mutual fund, which is my recommendation. Corporate bond funds will have a much greater yield than government bond funds. Caution! Do not tap into your IRA, because you will be charged a hefty penalty for a premature withdrawal. The IRS watches this like a hawk. Once you have secured another job, reevaluate your investment portfolio. You may consider reinvesting your bond dividends instead of moving them to a money market fund, or you may consider exiting the income-producing bond funds and purchasing equities.

Secure a Loan from Family Members

If all else fails and you really do need the cash to survive, seek a short-term loan from family members. Use this initiative as your last resort. Parents or grandparents are usually the best sources for personal loans. If you must go this route, prepare a formal written loan agreement stating the amount of the loan and the terms for repayment after you secure another job. Do not assume this is a family jackpot. Repay the loan on time.

MOVING FORWARD

The concern over financial matters after being let go does not stop here. We're talking about reducing risk through the purchase of insurance to protect against mishaps of every kind that cost money, sometimes *serious* money. In the next chapter I will walk you through the types of insurance that you will need, not only during your period of unemployment but also when you are employed again. Stick around.

CHAPTER TAKEAWAYS

- Seeking alternate income while unemployed is a common practice.
- Replacing income while unemployed is a short-term strategy, not a permanent solution.
- Frequently employers will hire back laid-off workers on an hourly or per-job basis.
- Tap into family money as a last resort.
- Do not tap into your IRA, because the penalties are extremely high.

DIGITAL AND PRINT RESOURCES

Social Security Administration, www.ssa.gov. Go to the search box and enter "unemployment benefits" for helpful information.

Unemployment Assist, www.unemployment-assist.com. This site provides assistance for accessing benefits.

Chapter 5

INSURANCE MATTERS: MEDICAL AND COBRA, DENTAL, HOMEOWNERS, AUTO, LIFE, DISABILITY

Insurance matters are of great importance, and all let-go workers must address them as soon as it is practicable. Life goes on after you lose your job, and *so do the risks that you face every day*. Untoward events never get laid off or take a vacation. On any given day, you could contract a life-threatening disease like pancreatic cancer, come down with a long-term debilitating and costly illness like Lyme disease, or you could have a car accident resulting in serious personal injury and substantial property damage. Your house or apartment is at risk, too. A hidden electrical malfunction could burn your dwelling to the ground and destroy all of your personal possessions in the process. Risk is omnipresent, and insurance is the only way to hedge against it. Many workers think insurance matters are boring, but when it comes to reducing risk, boring is good. In today's world, insurance has become a necessity.

Every person, regardless of social status or employment status, needs protection that insurance offers. The most important classes of insurance are: medical, dental, homeowners, automobile, life, long-term disability. Having adequate medical insurance is of the utmost importance for every laid-off worker and should be addressed when the termination takes place or shortly thereafter. We'll examine each classification beginning with medical insurance and the insurance option known as COBRA.

COBRA: THE CONSOLIDATED OMNIBUS BUDGET RECONCILIATION ACT

COBRA is a federal government program that enables workers to continue their medical insurance coverage after being let go. However, there are strict rules governing its implementation. For example, workers who are fired for gross misconduct are not eligible. Also, companies that employ fewer than twenty workers cannot participate in the plan.

While COBRA is a helpful risk-lowering federal government medical insurance plan, you must pay the entire cost of the plan plus an administrative fee after you are laid off. If your company group medical insurance premium was $5,000, split equally between you and your employer, now you are responsible for paying the *entire* premium plus a 2 percent administrative fee. Generally, you must apply for COBRA benefits within sixty days after being separated. Benefits will last for eighteen months and will cover you, your spouse, and your children. However, as with all government programs, the rules and regulations are constantly changing so act immediately if you elect to choose COBRA benefits. For other rules and regulations regarding COBRA, review the Department of Labor website.

Caution! Do not assume that you will find another job with medical insurance benefits and pass up the chance to use COBRA. Your period of unemployment could go on for six months or more and you cannot be without medical insurance for that long a period.

MEDICAL INSURANCE

Medical insurance is important for all workers but especially for laid off or fired workers whose COBRA coverage is coming to an end. You cannot risk being without medical insurance to cover costs for routine or extended care by a physician and costs for hospitalization.

Before your COBRA coverage expires, research individual medical insurance plans and be prepared to act. If you have no job prospects and COBRA is coming to an end, by all means purchase medical insurance for you and your dependents regardless of cost. Why? Tomorrow at this time you could be in the hospital with serious personal injury suffered in an accident. The natural tendency is to think, "It will never happen to me." That is nothing short of delusional. If you want verification for the uncertainty of life every day, just visit the emergency room at your local hospital. Sit in the waiting room for an hour or two and observe what happens. It will be a life-changing experience. Guaranteed.

Your options for purchasing medical insurance are limited by both state and federal rules and regulations. To determine what your options are, contact the human resources director at your former employer and the person in your doctor's office who handles insurance matters. Also, go online to research your options.

DENTAL INSURANCE

I speak from personal experience on this matter. One fine day, I was talking an early morning bike ride when I unexpectedly hit a patch of damp road. Down I went, striking my face on the pavement. The result? Two front teeth were cracked beyond repair and had to be replaced with dental implants. The cost? Five thousand dollars. And I had no dental insurance—an expensive mistake.

People often focus on health insurance and forget that it will not cover most dental work. Dental problems can arise without notice on any given day. We are always at risk for infections that require costly root canals, and for teeth damaged by accidents. For a realistic account of what can happen unexpectedly, talk with your dentist.

If you had dental coverage in your last job, by all means try to extend coverage while you are out of work. If you did not have it, go online and look for reasonably priced dental insurance. Most dental plans are limited to group coverage through an employer, but there are a handful of dental insurance companies offering individual plans.

HOMEOWNERS INSURANCE

When out of work, many workers try to minimize expenses by cutting insurance coverage on their homes or apartments. They say, "It will never happen to me. I'll cut my coverage while unemployed and pick it up after I get another job." Don't buy into that narrative. Homeowners carrying a mortgage do not have a choice because the mortgager requires coverage and, in most cases, it is factored into the monthly mortgage payment. However, if you own your property outright or live in an apartment, coverage is optional. Do not eliminate this coverage. On any given day, your residence could burn to the ground and take all of your belongings with it. On another given day, someone could trip over a rug in your apartment, fall, and incur serious personal injury. You will be responsible for payment of all medical expenses and possibly be sued for negligence. Homeowners insurance may seem optional when you are out of work, but it is not. It is a necessity in today's world.

AUTOMOBILE INSURANCE

Automobile insurance is required if your car is financed, and the premium is usually built into your monthly payment. In all states, proof of financial responsibility (i.e., automobile insurance) is required. You must present proof of coverage when you apply for or renew your license plates every year. Do not even think about skirting the rules and discontinuing premium payments believing that you will never get into an accident if you drive extra carefully. Once again, risk is with you 24/7. Automobile insurance is a necessity.

LIFE INSURANCE

"Why life insurance?" you might ask. "I'm in the prime of my life, and I'm not going to die in the foreseeable future." Think again. Your life could end at any time during the day or night, regardless of your age, leaving your dependents or extended family with expenses that could reach beyond their means. Burial expenses come to mind. Today, the average cost of a funeral, including the cemetery grave plot and headstone, is $13, 000, sometimes more. Add some upgrades like a fancy coffin and elaborate headstone, and the cost of your good-bye will run closer to $15,000.

The following true story illustrates the fact that life is risky and that death takes no holidays. It does not care if you are in mid-career and have children and a spouse, or that your income is an integral part of the family budget.

Linda's Story

I recruited Linda for a job as a reading consultant with an educational publisher where I was the regional sales manager for the Northeastern United States. Linda excelled in her job and was sought after by school districts implementing their new reading programs.

Linda belonged to a number of fine and performing arts organizations in Boston. She was an officer in the Junior League and performed volunteer work for the Museum of Fine Arts. Her teenage daughter was the pride and joy of her life and attended only the best schools.

As Linda entered mid-career, she and her husband frequently took skiing trips to Aspen and Vail in addition to vacations in Europe and the Caribbean. Life was good for Linda. In February 2008, they went on a five-day ski trip to Vail and returned home tired and happy. However, Linda seemed more tired than usual after five days on the slopes and scheduled an appointment with her doctor to see if she needed a dose of vitamins to keep up her energy level. As a precaution, Linda's doctor ordered lab tests and an abdominal CT scan. He called these tests "routine." However, the "routine" tests indicated that Linda had pancreatic cancer. Surgery followed and so did death, seven weeks after diagnosis. Linda possessed intelligence, energy, and passion beyond the ordinary, but death does not play favorites. To this day, Linda is missed by her husband, daughter, friends, and coworkers. They still ask, "How could she have died in the prime of her life without forewarning?" Rest in peace, Linda.

There are several forms of life insurance. The most common, and the lowest in price, is called "term life insurance," which is what most employers provide for their employees. It terminates as soon as you are fired or laid off. When you walk out the door after being let go, you are no longer insured. Purchasing term life insurance should be a priority for all let-go workers. It is readily available from any number of life insurance companies at reasonable cost for mid-career workers. Conduct an online search for low-cost term life insurance and purchase it immediately.

LONG-TERM DISABILITY INSURANCE (LTD)

The story goes something like this. "I don't need LTD insurance because 'it' will never happen to me." Most of us delude ourselves into thinking that accidents resulting in long-term or permanent disability always happen to the other guy. I fell into this trap in mid-career, too, and but for the guidance of an extraordinary insurance saleswoman, I would not have survived financially.

Chicken Man

I was riding my bike past a farm is a rural section of Bucks County, Pennsylvania. Suddenly, a bantam chicken darted from weeds growing along the side of the road into the front wheel of my bike, and down I went. I suffered a concussion, a torn rotator cuff, and a fractured hip and was disabled for eight months following surgery and a two-week stay in the hospital. During this time, I had no income, but the bills kept rolling in: mortgage payments, car payments, property taxes, and college tuition bills for the children. I survived only because my insurance agent, Joanne, had badgered me into purchasing LTD insurance. The policy became effective just a week before the accident and provided income to survive this ordeal. Thank you, Joanne, for educating me about risks we face each day when we get out of bed.

Many insurers provide LTD coverage, but most are group plans for employers. Two companies that provide individual LTD insurance are Northwestern Mutual and Unum. Go online and check out their LTD options and prices.

MOVING FORWARD

Most people consider insurance a boring topic, one to be avoided at all cost. The unexpected illness or accident always happens to someone else. Don't fool yourself. Consider the insurances detailed above as much a necessity as food, shelter, and clothing. In today's world, you cannot live without it. Insurance is a family matter, too, as it protects those dear to you not only from temporary financial challenges, but also from catastrophic loss.

There is something else you must do concurrently to ensure your future employability. It is something that most laid-off workers bypass entirely because there is so much going on. I'm talking about your reputation, which will be the subject of the next chapter, "Safeguarding Your Reputation."

CHAPTER TAKEAWAYS

- Apply for COBRA medical insurance immediately after being separated from your company.
- Consider purchasing a private medical insurance policy as an alternative to COBRA, which is available to you for only eighteen months after termination.
- Death and accidents take no holidays.
- According to the National Highway Traffic Administration, an automobile accident occurs every sixty seconds.
- LTD and life insurance are equally important for mid-career workers.

PRINT AND DIGITAL RESOURCES

For detailed information on COBRA, see www.COBRAinsurance. com.

For current information about disability insurance policies, see www.insure.com/disability-insurance.

Chapter 6

SAFEGUARDING YOUR REPUTATION

Reputation is one of your most valuable possessions, and it is in your best interest to safeguard it after being let go. Word travels fast through social media, email, and phone messages. Even before you are officially notified that you are being laid off, your boss and the human resources manager know what is happening. And so does everyone in their respective networks, like the company president and CEO.

The reason for your layoff usually involves company finances. When a company needs to show better bottom line, frequently workers are eliminated. It has nothing to do with your work ethic or personal behavior, but when colleagues see you walk out the door escorted by a guard, they might assume the worst.

RUMORS SPREAD QUICKLY

With so many people knowing that you have been let go, rumors can spread fast about the reason for your departure. Speculation abounds. Human nature being what it is, some of that speculation could reflect negatively on your reputation. Idle chatter could go something like this:

- "Wonder why Mary got axed. Bet it was because she was late for work so many times."

- "Seems that Bob's home remodeling business always left something to be desired. Remember when his workers left the house in a mess after installing the kitchen cabinets?"
- "Her interpersonal skills were not so great. She always seemed to say something that ticked off the boss. I guess they did not feel she was trustworthy."

Before long, idle talk could tarnish your personal and professional reputation and impede your chances of finding another job. To head off any assaults on your reputation, time is of the essence.

STRATEGIES FOR PROTECTING YOUR REPUTATION

Preemptive strikes are the best way to quash rumors that could begin inadvertently or by design from detractors. Here are some strategies to begin the process of protecting what you have worked so hard to achieve.

Termination Letters

The dismissal event usually catches workers off guard. They gather their personal possessions and walk out the door, never even thinking about having the boss and the human resources director state the reason for dismissal in a written termination letter. If you did not receive a termination letter, contact your former human resources director and request a signed termination letter that includes the following items:

- Your name
- The beginning date of your employment and the date of termination
- Specific reasons for termination, like a major company reorganization, reduction in force because of economic conditions, sale of the company, or any other reason that caused your position to be eliminated
- Signature of the human resources director

The termination letter is an important document to keep in your personal files as verification for the reasons why your job was eliminated. When applying for a new job, you may want to present the termination letter along with your resume.

Letters of Recommendation

When requesting your termination letter, always ask for a letter of recommendation signed by your former boss and/or the human resources director. Usually they will be more than obliging if the request is made in conjunction with your being let go or shortly thereafter while your good work is still fresh in their minds. There is a certain amount of sympathy for a terminated worker, and on most occasions the former boss will honor your request. However, your request may be denied or forgotten if you wait months to act, so do it now.

Frequently, letters of recommendation, or letters of reference as they are sometimes called, are nothing more than happy talk. They say nothing meaningful about who you are and what you can do professionally. The letter should address two traits: your public image (your *persona*) and your personal traits (your *character*). When you request someone to write a letter of recommendation, suggest that the letter address the following points about your character and persona:

- Trustworthiness
- Your industry and company reputation
- That you abided by the rules established by your employer
- Punctuality
- Physical and mental energy level
- Passion for completing any task on time
- Ability to get along with subordinates and superiors
- Leadership skills

These are the personality and character points that every prospective employer examines when evaluating you for a job.

We suggest that you acquire additional letters of recommendation or reference from company coworkers and customers you have worked with. Timeliness is of the essence, as memories fade quickly. Strike while the iron is hot and request these letters as soon as possible after being terminated.

Protecting Your Online Reputation

When prospective employers see your name in a list of candidates for a specific job, the first thing they do is Google your name to learn more about you personally and professionally. Usually the first stop is LinkedIn, to compare what they see on your resume with your online profile. Start the process by asking workers in your network to provide a LinkedIn recommendation attesting to your character traits and work expertise. Don't hesitate to ask your contacts to address specific traits that you want potential employers to notice.

If you have not yet done so, update your LinkedIn profile. Provide the dates you were employed with your last employer and add the heading "Accomplishments at Saturn Software, Inc.," followed by three or four key items. For example, a regional sales manager wants everyone to know that she attained or surpassed her sales goals. State that accomplishment like this: "Exceeded multimillion-dollar revenue goals for the past five years in my twelve-state region while managing a staff of fifteen outbound, full-time sales representatives."

Making a Graceful Exit

While the layoff is hurtful in the extreme, being let go provides an opportunity to enhance your character and reputation. Soon after leaving the company, send a thank-you letter or email to your boss, the human resources director, and the president. It could go something like this: "Leaving was very difficult, but I enjoyed my stay with the company, and thank you for giving me the opportunity to learn and grow in my career. When you have another opportunity, I would appreciate your keeping me in mind. I wish your company the best going forward."

You want your former employer to think and speak well of you personally and professionally. It does you no good whatsoever to maintain a negative attitude toward your former employer. Your former boss or president could move on to another company and be the hiring manager when you apply for work with that employer. Never burn bridges.

MOVING FORWARD

In addition to protecting finances and reputation, the mid-career worker faces additional challenges related to family issues that could prove distracting and add an additional burden to the budget. We'll identify family challenges and offer solutions in the next chapter.

CHAPTER TAKEAWAYS

- Do not trash your former employer.
- Have your former boss or human resources director write a termination letter specifying the reason for your departure.
- Ask colleagues to post positive reviews about your work on LinkedIn.
- Solicit letters of recommendation from your previous employer and from colleagues as soon as possible after being let go.

PRINT AND DIGITAL RESOURCES

"How To Manage (and Protect) Your Online Reputation." *Forbes*. www.forbes.com. Go to the website and enter the title of this article in the search box.

Chapter 7

FAMILY CHALLENGES AND SOLUTIONS

Our workforce is almost evenly divided between men and women. Both face the same workplace challenges and both are subject to losing their jobs periodically throughout their careers. Approximately 55,000 workers lose their jobs every day, and, contrary to popular opinion, women and men lose their jobs at the same rate. When employers need to shed personnel, gender is not an issue.

Women and men face similar challenges after being let go. The issues frequently center on childcare, aging-parent care, separation or divorce, and education. Let's examine each challenge and explore solutions.

THE CHILDCARE CHALLENGE

When a parent is laid off, family lifestyle is altered because of childcare responsibilities. Even though there might be a continuing income stream coming from a spouse's job, something has to give. Expenses across the board must be adjusted. Usually, the person at home, the husband or wife, picks up the slack. Caring for kids is a time-consuming process that begins when they wake up and get ready for school and continues until they finish homework and go to bed. Adding these responsibilities to the process of finding another job is frustrating because there are only so many hours in a day. The parent looking for another job has resumes and cover letters to write, personal interviews away from home that might require an overnight stay, phone interviews, networking calls, attendance at trade shows or job fairs, and the list goes on. Looking for a job is a full-time job in itself, but when added to caring for the children, the challenge to make it work can be overwhelming.

Specific challenges include transporting children to and from school, making sure they complete homework assignments, meeting with teachers to discuss the children's progress or problems, and driving them to and from recreational events. All of these responsibilities are in addition to caring for their day-to-day physical and emotional needs. So how does the laid-off parent handle childcare responsibilities and look for employment concurrently?

The Childcare Solution

Nothing happens without a plan. Your first initiative in solving this problem should be to sit down at your computer or notepad and make an hourly written plan that you can refer to every day. Block out those hours you will spend seeking new employment, even if it means letting household chores take a back seat. If your spouse has questions about how you can care for the kids while job hunting, construct a plan for him or her to pick up the slack. The employed spouse might not like doing routine childcare chores like driving the kids to school and that is understandable. But you are in this together. Construct a plan that is equitable for both.

During this unemployment hiatus, you can't possibly do it all yourself. What happens when you are going to a trade show or meeting with a network contact, or when you go to an interview? Again, we get back to the plan. When it is necessary to leave the house, you will need a backup to handle the childcare responsibilities. The key is to plan for these outside-the-home events at least a week in advance. Seek help from your spouse, neighbors, friends, parents, or grandparents. Most people, including your spouse, are willing to lend a hand to someone in need as long as the request for help is on a timely basis. When you need help, say so.

If you can't resolve the childcare issues with "free" help, sit down with your spouse and make a financial plan that includes paying for outside help with the children. This could mean a reallocation of discretionary dollars to childcare dollars, which may be uncomfortable, but remember that this is temporary. When you find another job, you can reconstruct your budget to include formal childcare payments.

Some laid-off workers with considerable childcare responsibilities elect to seek employment that can be done *at home*, a very attractive alternative to full-time work away from home. In fact, a report by the National Bureau of Economic Research revealed that the average worker values working from home and is willing to give up about 10 percent of their wages to exercise this option.

THE AGING PARENT CHALLENGE

All of us can cite examples where a mid-career worker is faced with caring for an aging parent or a parent who has developed a debilitating illness such as Alzheimer's. Unfortunately, illness has no respect for your time or the fact that you are temporarily unemployed.

The Aging Parent Solution

When the unemployed spouse has this responsibility in addition to shouldering some of the childcare responsibilities and is looking for a new job, there are not enough hours in the day to get it all done. Something has to give. Other family members must help the unemployed person make all of the moving parts come together.

If the parent in need is at home and requires transportation to and from the doctor or hospital, build that into your plan. If this is in conflict with your eighth-grade son's basketball schedule, he may need to cut some practice sessions or competitive games. It's a good opportunity to counsel your son that taking care of family members is everyone's responsibility. Bring him into the picture by prioritizing events in order of importance. Counsel him that caring for a family member comes before basketball, no exceptions.

If the aging-parent situation becomes too time-consuming while you are unemployed and looking for new full-time opportunities, a viable solution is to seek only part-time employment. (According to research conducted by the Pew Research Center, 27 percent of the respondents surveyed said they left their full-time jobs permanently to care for an ill parent or child.) Implementing this alternative could make all the moving parts—parent care, childcare, income stream, work-life balance—work together.

THE DIVORCE OR SEPARATION CHALLENGE

While exiting an unhappy marriage is a liberating experience, it can pose a challenge for a mid-career worker who has been fired or laid off. When this event occurs, two factors come into play: dealing with the trauma accompanying divorce and dealing with the trauma of losing a job. It's a double challenge, but there are solutions.

The Divorce/Separation Solution

A top priority for divorced or separated laid-off workers is to maintain self-confidence. Such workers need to reaffirm their ability to move forward and rebuild their career into something that will provide income, job satisfaction, and work-life balance, all while trying to sort out the divorce or separation.

The best way to find a job while divorced or separated, and avoid depression, is to leave the house and attend trade shows at nearby convention centers. There you will find hundreds of potential employers under one roof and opportunities to make new friends, build your professional network, and expand your work horizons. Even if the trade show is not focusing on your area of expertise or interest, attend just the same. A new environment frequently reveals interests and abilities never before imagined.

But what about the divorce itself? Dealing with a double whammy, divorce and job loss, is a real bummer because both are calling for your attention. We suggest focusing on the job first because in our culture, a job confers self-esteem and a sense of identity, both of which are necessary to resolve uncomfortable issues. When you have a job, even a job that is not exactly what you would like, you will be better able to work through the divorce or separation with confidence and resolve. When you are out of work you are just plain vanilla James Jones. When you have a job, you are James Jones, Director of Marketing for Ajax Software. There is a world of difference. A job with a title and a paycheck confer self-esteem, respect, dignity, and financial independence.

MOVING FORWARD

Even though various family responsibilities and job-hunting activities are time-consuming, use this period of unemployment to begin improving your character and redefining your persona. Allot a certain amount of time each day for this project. This is an interesting task in the rebuilding process, and we'll help you with it in the next chapter. Keep reading.

CHAPTER TAKEAWAYS

- Family responsibilities continue after being laid off. Plan accordingly.
- Childcare, aging parents, and divorce/separation present challenges, but by using your intelligence, energy, and creativity, you can find solutions.
- Part-time jobs frequently offer a viable temporary solution when a laid-off worker is overwhelmed with family-care responsibilities.
- Sales jobs frequently offer flexible hours and work schedules.
- After losing your job, create a daily agenda to meet your responsibilities.
- Plan your work. Work your plan.

PRINT AND DIGITAL RESOURCES

Best Companies for Working Mothers. www.workingmother.com/best-companies.

Morris, Virginia and Jennie Hansen. *How to Care for Aging Parents: A One-Stop Resource for All of Your Medical, Financial, Housing, and Emotional Needs.* 3rd edition. Workman Publishing Co, 2014.

Part II

THE PROCESS OF MOVING FORWARD IN YOUR CAREER

Believe in yourself! Have faith in your abilities! Without a humble but reasonable confidence in your own powers you cannot be successful or happy.

—Norman Vincent Peale

Chapter 8

RESHAPING YOUR PERSONA AND IMPROVING YOUR CHARACTER

We develop our character and persona over time without thinking about who we are becoming. Character traits are something learned from first influencers, parents, and teachers. We develop our persona as we grow and present ourselves to the public. We seldom realize that these traits are what lead us to do what we do and how we do it. Often we settle into patterns and do not reflect on them. For example, you may have been at your last job for a number of years and after two promotions, your interest waned, and going to work each day became a chore. It seemed that your head was somewhere else, but you could not determine why. Then one day you were laid off in a massive company reorg and you asked, "What am I going to do now? My last job put bread on the table and gave me status and respectability, but I did not like it, and it never felt like the right fit. There has to be a better way."

Being fired or laid off is traumatic, but it does have benefits, two of which are:

1. It opens the door to reviewing and possibly reshaping your persona.
2. It provides an opportunity to learn who you really are by examining your character.

RESHAPING YOUR PERSONA

The word *persona* derives from the Latin where it originally referred to a theatrical mask. In theatrical terms, it is an assumed personality. In today's world, it refers to that part of your personality exposed to the public. It is the *apparent* you that people see, and it may be different from your character, the *real* you. It is you who created your persona, either consciously or subconsciously and it may have resulted in your being a dynamic leader or a loyal follower.

People in the public eye such as company presidents or CEOs, TV personalities, actors, and politicians, frequently assume a certain persona that appeals to their target audience. Take politicians, for example. They want to be viewed by constituents as caring for their welfare and the needs of the country as a whole, but sometimes their character flaws are revealed and they fall from grace. The disconnect between the two, once it has emerged into the public view, can lead to the politician's being perceived as unreliable and dishonest.

Persona is equally important in the private sector. Let's review the persona of a well-known deceased CEO, Steve Jobs, cofounder and CEO of Apple Computer. When I worked with Apple in its early days, Steve's persona was that of the good, kind, caring, and generous boss. However, behind his mask, Steve could be a ruthless guy, one who might greet you in the morning and say a polite "Good Morning" or look at you with fury in his eyes and say, "You're fired!" for no apparent reason. Nobody quite knew who Steve really was, and for that reason many workers left Apple or declined offers to work there.

Bring this to a more personal level and look at your persona in the workplace. Focus on the role you played in your last job, the one that disappeared one day when you were least expecting it. If you were in a leadership position (i.e., the boss), what was your persona? Was it in conflict with the real you? Did you think of yourself as the good, compassionate, helpful, caring boss dedicated to making the company great? Did you assume this persona, this mask, to hide your real motivation: to oust your boss and move up in rank and compensation? Could it have been the reason why you were let go from your job as regional sales manager in a staged "reorganization" while your friend Mary, another regional sales manager, was kept on the payroll? Only you can answer that after a private, honest meeting with yourself.

Before making the big move toward serious job hunting, discover who you really are. Were you the one who used every chance to derail your boss while playing Mister Good Guy? If your introspection reveals a difference between your persona and the real you, take measures to make these two competing entities one and the same. How do you begin? With honesty. If you have any doubts about how you are seen, ask your former boss and coworkers what they thought of you, no holds barred.

IMPROVING YOUR CHARACTER

Character can be defined as the aggregate of traits and features that form and identify the real you. Your character is the set of values and sense of ethics that you hold dear. They determine not only what you might say, but also how you act.

This period of downtime affords an opportunity not only to see where you've been and where you want to go, but also to learn who you really are now that you can't hide behind a corporate title or affiliation. Looking back, you might find that the real you became lost in the corporate culture, or was disguised by a preoccupation with political correctness. In the course of your previous job, you may have forgotten what you truly think or how you feel. It's time for a homecoming with yourself to find out who you really are.

To begin the process of rebuilding character, you need a foundation upon which everything else rests. I like best the foundation stones posited by Character Counts!, a nonprofit organization dedicated to character education. One of their constructs is the Six Pillars of Character, which act as the foundation for exploring character education and character building. These pillars are: trustworthiness, fairness, respect, caring, citizenship, and responsibility. Review this material at: www.charactercounts.org.

The next step is to determine who you truly want to be and how you can build character traits to fulfill your mission. For example, assume that your goal is to secure a leadership position in a management job where you can help your staff grow professionally by acquiring new skills and by working as a team. This mission requires you to develop character traits that include teaching and mentoring skills, learning how to assess an individual's strengths and weaknesses, accepting total responsibility for your role in the company, and becoming a sympathetic listener.

The rebuilding process is not for the timid. The easiest path is to do nothing and just hope that *something* will happen in the future. Chose this path, and you will stay where you are now, the same old you who lost a job quite possibly because you did not have those character traits to be an effective leader or a loyal and productive follower.

MOVING FORWARD

Redefining your persona and improving your character will prepare you to move forward with confidence to the next phase of the rebuilding process, establishing objectives for the remainder of your career. It's just ahead in the next chapter.

CHAPTER TAKEAWAYS

- Persona is the face you present to the public at large.
- Character is who you really are.
- Persona and character must work in harmony for growth in your new career.

PRINT AND DIGITAL RESOURCES

Brooks, David. *The Road to Character*. Random House, 2016.
Character Counts! www.charactercounts.org.

Chapter 9

DEFINING OBJECTIVES FOR THE REMAINDER OF YOUR CAREER

Recently I reviewed the resume of an interesting mid-career worker. Under "Professional Employment," which covered the past five years, I saw "US Peace Corps, English Teacher." Following that was a string of twelve jobs in different industries spanning twenty years. It was one year here, six months there, two years at a different company, and so on. When I interviewed this candidate, he told me he had been fired from the last corporate job he held as associate marketing manager for a publishing company. This was the catalyst that prompted him to embark on an extended period of reflection to find his real self. As a result, he learned that he was driven not by status, power, and money as so many workers are in the for-profit corporate world. His new objective was to be instrumental in the lives of people studying to reach their full potential. After a period of introspection, he decided that the ideal job to accomplish that objective was teaching. He took online courses that awarded teaching certification and subsequently found work with the Peace Corps. The job provided enough money for him to be self-sufficient and gave him the sense of mission he had been seeking. Making the transition from the Peace Corps to the "civilian" world was easy for this candidate. He found a job teaching at a local high school. The objective he established after his last corporate job provided direction for the remainder of his career.

Many mid-career workers who have been let go worked in one industry in similar departments, like sales or marketing, for the first half of their careers. For example, take Claudia, a mid-career woman who came to me seeking help finding new employment after losing her job. She was working in the pharmaceutical industry since attaining her BS in biology. All of her jobs were in sales or marketing. The money was good, but the job satisfaction was zero. When she was let go in a reorganization, Claudia thought about her work history and realized that she did not like working in sales and marketing, so she asked, "What's next? More of the same? How can I get out of this sales and marketing game and still make enough money to survive?" During her period of introspection, she learned that she really did not care for the business world. Going after the sale was not in line with her character. She was caring and compassionate and had the ability to impart information objectively. She remembered that her first love was teaching others about the world of living things, biology. She went back to school, online and at a bricks-and-mortar college, and earned a minor in education, which qualified her for a public school teaching position. After teaching biology at a local high school, Claudia found a job as an editor with an educational publishing company where she works now editing high school science texts and digital materials. She is not making as much money as she did on the corporate side, but she earns enough to live a comfortable life, and she has something that money cannot buy—job satisfaction. For workers like Claudia, being fired or laid off is often a blessing in disguise because it gives one time to pause, reflect, and reset before moving forward to another career.

SEARCHING FOR CAREER OBJECTIVES

Redefining your career goals is a process that you can accomplish in the classroom of your own mind. You do not need multiple sessions with a shrink, nor do you need to attend every conference advertised by motivational speakers trumpeting, "Find Yourself in Three Easy Steps." You have the intelligence and energy to accomplish this mission yourself. Here are strategies to begin the self-defining process.

Four Steps in the Redefining Process

1. Write your career vision statement, one that defines what you
    believe will fulfill career expectations. It might read like this:
    Moving forward in the second half of my working years, I
    wish to find a career that combines my interests with my
    aptitudes and abilities, and that will provide income to sus-
    tain a middle-class style of living.

2. On a sheet of physical or digital paper, draw two lines down
    the middle of the page to create three columns. Title the left-
    hand column "My Interests" and make a list of five things that
    interest you most. One word or a phrase is sufficient. For ex-
    ample, your first five written entries may be:
    Music, primarily show tunes;
    Sports, especially baseball;
    Finance, especially insurance;
    Laws/rules/regulations that make for a safe and secure
    America;
    Environmental conservation to create a clean and healthful
    climate.

3. Title the middle column on your page "My Aptitudes/Exper-
    tise." Beside each of your five interests, write your aptitude
    and experience corresponding to each of your five interests.

4. Title the right-hand column, the third column, "Jobs." Record
    a job corresponding to your interests and abilities in the first
    and second columns.

Assume that your primary interest is in the broadly defined field
of environmental conservation, but you don't know what jobs are
available in this field. You can go to the Internet to conduct a search,
or you can consult the online or print version of one of the best
sources available for career information. It was developed by the
United States Department of Labor and job seekers have purchased
millions of copies. It is revised every year and is available from booksellers like Amazon and Barnes & Noble. It is the *Occupational*
Outlook Handbook, which is cited below under "Print and Digital

Resources." Look for jobs in your area of interest, environmental conservation. You will find them in the sections titled "Green Occupations," "Education," and "Life/Physical/Social Science." Each section lists related occupations, the forecast for such jobs, education and skill requirements, advancement opportunities, work environment, and average earnings. The thousand-page *OOH* is a valuable resource for workers redefining their career goals. Have a copy near at hand while exploring new career paths. After consulting the *OHH*, your record sheet might look something like this:

My Interests	My Aptitudes/Experience	Jobs
Environmental Conservation	Audubon Society Volunteer Work	Ecologist, Teacher

Searching for Employers Who Meet Your Objectives

Following this exercise, search for employers who offer jobs in environmental conservation. The most expeditious way to find a plethora of such companies is to conduct a Google search. Enter "companies with jobs in environmental conservation." When I did that, I found numerous employers active in such pursuits. Some of those were: CWM Environmental, Watts Architecture and Engineering, North Cascades Institute, Packaging Corporation of America, and State of North Carolina.

For additional prompts on opportunities in the field of environmental conservation—or whatever field you might be interested in—consider federal government jobs, which are often overlooked by workers seeking new career goals. To begin the process, we recommend consulting what is considered the bible of government jobs, *The Book of U.S. Government Jobs: Where They Are, What's Available, and How to Complete a Federal Resume*. Expand the process by reviewing the corresponding website: www.federaljobs.net. When I reviewed the book, I found an interesting reference to the "Environmental and Natural Resources Division" of the US Department of Justice. This Division develops and enforces civil environmental laws that protect US natural resources.

When you have found posted job opportunities with an employer who meets your objectives, continue the process by establishing a relationship with the hiring manager for the position that interests you or with the human resources director. Present your candidacy for the position of interest using the rubrics in this book for resume writing, interviewing, and negotiating a job offer.

CONTINUING IN YOUR PRESENT CAREER PATH

Not every laid-off worker seeks a new career path. Many wish to continue working in their present careers, but with an employer who provides opportunities for work-life balance, community outreach initiatives, and job satisfaction. Such workers can move directly to seeking potential job opportunities in their chosen industry. For example, a worker in the food industry who had been working in managerial positions with fast-food providers may now look for more health-conscious companies in the food industry like Whole Foods or Wegmans.

Workers in the technology industry frequently reach a point where they need more than a big paycheck and less than a sixty-hour work week. Take one of my family members, Andrew, for example. He was riffed from his tech company where he had nine direct reports and worked long hours. He wanted to remain in technology and used his downtime to find employers engaged in a socially conscious business. After almost a year of searching, he hit pay dirt with a national pharmacy company. In his new job Andrew supervises a department using robotic technology to fill prescriptions for people needing continuous refills of life-sustaining medications. He manages the entire process using his many technology skills and takes home not only a paycheck, but also job satisfaction resulting from his work in a life-sustaining business.

WHERE AM I GOING?

Now that you are ready to activate your search for another job, what can you expect? Based on my experience working with let-go workers and anecdotal reports, I predict that three to six months from now you will be gainfully employed in one of four ways.

Four Options for Future Employment

1. Employment with a company in an industry you like and that pays more than your previous position.
2. Employment in a *meaningful* job that brings you personal satisfaction in addition to an income that provides for your needs.
3. Employment as an entrepreneur by starting your own business.
4. Employment as a worker in an entirely different industry pursuing what you always wanted to do but could never before find the courage to try.

MOVING FORWARD

Now that you have diligently used your intelligence and skills to define your objectives, you are ready for the next step in the process, crafting a resume that reflects the *new you*. The following chapter will guide you through the resume-writing process.

CHAPTER TAKEAWAYS

*   Redefine career objectives on your own or with the help of resources like the *Occupational Outlook Handbook*.
*   A meaningful career provides job satisfaction in addition to power, status, and money.
*   Workers can transfer work skills from one industry to another.

PRINT AND DIGITAL RESOURCES

Damp, Dennis. *The Book of U.S. Government Jobs*. Bookhaven Press, 2011.

Federal Government Jobs. www.federaljobs.net.

The US Department of Labor. *Occupational Outlook Handbook*. JIST Publishing, 2016-2017.

Chapter 10

CRAFTING A RESUME AND DIGITAL PROFILE TO REFLECT THE *NEW YOU*

Crafting a new resume is not everyone's idea of a good time. In fact, I have witnessed many mid-career workers struggle with this task because they have not updated their resumes for five years. The resume created five or more years ago does not include your recent accomplishments. Adding these accomplishments and additional information, like professional development, education, and community outreach activities, gives you an entirely new look. It is really a new you in writing. In addition, crafting a new digital profile for LinkedIn should be a concurrent effort. The digital profile and the resume must be in sync because potential employers and executive recruiters review both items.

THE PURPOSE OF A RESUME

You craft a resume in order to interest a potential employer in your candidacy and to motivate the hiring manager to schedule a personal interview. However, no matter how great your resume, if it does not get to the right person your candidacy will go nowhere. Many job candidates sit at home and send resumes by the hundreds to job boards and company career pages. The result? Nothing.

Companies do not hire resumes. They hire living, breathing, walking, talking, thinking candidates who have the smarts to leave the house and meet hiring managers and human resources directors, in the flesh, to begin building a relationship.

GENERAL GUIDELINES FOR WRITING YOUR RESUME

Job candidates frequently spend hundreds of hours writing the *perfect* resume based upon advice from peers, spouses, college professors, and a variety of online resources. When you say "resume," everyone provides suggestions and advice believing their way is the best way. While some of this input could have value, most of it is redundant or based on personal experience, which may be outdated. Even college professors get into the act and give advice that has no relevance in the business world. For example, they call the resume *curriculum vitae*, a term used only by the academic establishment. Do not refer to your resume as a CV. In the business world, it is a *resume*.

Resume guidelines vary with the times. Today's resume has certain major components and a certain style. Gone are the days of block paragraphs to describe previous jobs and their responsibilities.

My experiences as an executive recruiter working in the staffing industry every day is the basis for the direction I offer. If you follow my instructions, you will design a first-class resume that reflects what is current and acceptable in today's business world. However, if you want general resume-writing advice, review websites like Career Confidential, www.careerconfidential.com. The CEO, Peggy McKee, is one of the best in the business, and I suggest that you attend one of her many webinars, the cost of which is very attractive—*free*.

What about those professional resume-writing services that charge $50 to $300 for designing your resume? If these resume-writing gurus sell their services, they must be good. Right? Save your money. Spend that money to attend a trade show or conference where you will find hundreds of hiring managers in person. This would be money well spent because landing a job is a matter of building a personal relationship with hiring managers and other influential company workers like the director of human resources.

Still, there are some rules and guidelines that are important to keep in mind. I have reviewed thousands of resumes in my recruiting business. Few are outstanding; many are just okay; and some are too cute. Cute resumes contain too many unnecessary stylistic features like a nonstandard typeface, multiple colors, clip art, photos, borders, and other design features. The basic rule is this: *Keep it simple. Keep it clean.* Remember this is business communication, not a promotion piece for the Super Bowl and certainly not a menu for a French restaurant.

Recruiters working in the staffing business know how a resume should look, and they can tell you what mistakes to avoid. Executive recruiters say these are the five most common mistakes candidates make on resumes:

Five Common Resume Mistakes

1. *Typos.* Correct spelling is your responsibility, not the spell-checker's. Nothing will send your resume to the trash heap faster than a misspelled word.

2. *Grammar mistakes.* Hiring managers expect grammatically correct resumes from everyone. Make a mistake, and you are finished. There is no second chance.

3. *Inconsistent formatting and style.* Use only one typeface and type size. The current preferred typeface is 12 pt. Times New Roman.

4. *Missing metrics.* Quantify as much as possible. Generalities say nothing about your expertise or accomplishments.

5. *Gaps in employment history.* You do have a work history, which consists of full-time professional experience and possibly significant part-time work in college or even high school. Make sure your work history is in chronological order beginning with your last job and going back to your first job.

RESUME FEATURES YOU MUST GET RIGHT

One could write pages listing the most important rubrics for resume writing. Do this. Don't do that. Do it this way. No, do it my way. It's not that complicated. Here are the items you must get right to produce a credible resume:

- *Resume File Name.* This is one of the most important parts of your resume and you must get it right. The file name must be brief and to the point so the reader will understand without hesitation who you are and what the file is about. State the file name like this:

  "Jerome Michael's Resume. Marketing Associate Candidate for General Electric."

- *Resume Length.* The resume for an entry-level candidate and a resume for a mid-career candidate will differ in length. Appearance, style, and format, however, are the same for all candidates. Length of resume for all entry-level candidates should be no more than two pages. However, the resumes for mid-career workers with ten to twenty years of experience that includes executive-level positions and possibly publications could be three or four pages, or even more.

- *Resume Appearance.* Your resume is your personal appearance in written form. Think of it as the way you would dress for a live interview: uncluttered and neat. Hiring managers are not interested in your picture, graphs, boxed items, borders, charts, shading, or clip art. If they want to see how you look, they can always go to LinkedIn, Facebook, Twitter, or other social media.

- *Resume Formatting.* Consistency is key from beginning to end. Use bullet points consisting of only one line instead of paragraphs in the body of the resume. Use only one typeface and size. Use uppercase bold for major headings and lowercase regular type for text. Do not use a script typeface, like *Segoe Script,* under any circumstances. The typeface is not the tool to differentiate your candidacy from the rest of the pack.

- *Resume Style.* Resume styles change over time. Today's readers view content in small bits and pieces. They lose interest when confronted with long paragraphs. Save that for your first novel. The way we convey information is by using bullet points instead of paragraphs, with one exception. The first major heading of your resume, "Objective" or "Summary," should be in paragraph form but not to exceed about ten lines. List every other item in bullet points. Use "Objective" when you are applying for a specific job. Use "Summary" if you are submitting your resume to a human resources director to make this key person aware of your search for an unspecified position in the company.

- *Resume Metrics.* One of the most common mistakes candidates make is listing their achievements using broad generalities like, "Treated a large number of patients at the emergency room at Chicago Hospital." The statement means much more to the hiring manager if it reads, "Treated an average of thirty patients per day over a three-year period at Chicago Hospital."

MAJOR HEADINGS OF YOUR RESUME

Here are the major parts of your resume. Include all of them on your resume in this order.

1. Personal Identification
2. Objective or Summary
3. Military Work Experience (if applicable)
4. Work Experience
5. Awards, Recognition, Community Service
6. Technology Skills
7. Education

Do not include "References on Request" or "Hobbies and Special Interests." Here is a review of each major heading with an explanatory note.

Personal Identification

The first items on your resume, at the top of the page and centered, are your name, address, phone number, and email address. Use only one phone number, the one that you use most frequently for both inbound and outbound calls. Remember that calls regarding employment matters come at all hours. The 9:00 a.m. to 5:00 p.m. window is no longer valid. Your address must include your street number, town, and zip code. Your name should be first, in uppercase bold. Beneath your name is the address, phone number, and email address in lowercase regular type.

I have received resumes without an address, only a name, phone number, Twitter hashtag, and an email address. This is the result of a mistaken notion of tech gurus who believe that in a digital world where you live is not important. Tell that to a human resources director, and you are history. Do not buy into the hype. Use common sense. Always include your full address.

Objective or Summary

This is nothing more than a marketing piece about the product you are selling: your candidacy. Write this in paragraph format and limit your self-advertisement to ten lines. Write a custom "Objective" for each job application reflecting the contents and requirements in the job description. Specifically, state your work expertise in terms that reflect the job specifications and using key words from the job description. Remember that the reader, the hiring manager or the human resources director, is thinking, "What can this person do for our team and the company going forward?"

If there is only a general statement on a company website under "careers" that reads, "Customer Service Representative Manager," think about what this position requires: excellent verbal and written skills, patience, punctuality, understanding, and courtesy. Build your objective statement around the job description.

State specifically the position for which you are applying (e.g., "I am applying for the Finance Manager position."). If appropriate, quantify your experience. For example, if you are applying for a position requiring writing skills, state, "My written communication experience includes ten years as housing industry writer for *Forbes* magazine." In your cover letter, you can elaborate on that experience.

In this section, you may want to include specific competencies in a list of single words or phrases following the "Objective" or "Summary" paragraph. Here is an example.

> *Core Competencies*
> *PowerPoint   Excel   Database   Social Media*
> *Personnel Management   Field Manual Writing*
> *Logistics   Editing   Research*

Including such a list will give you a plus mark if the company is using key-word scanning software.

Military Work Experience (only if applicable)

List your military experience chronologically beginning with your most recent service assignment and rank. List each MOS (Military Occupation Specialty) under a major heading followed by specifics in bullet point format. Do not use acronyms and write using civilian-speak, not military jargon.

Work Experience

Make this a chronological listing beginning with your most recent work experience. To explain what you did at these companies, state your responsibilities in bullet point format. In the following example, note that each contains a specific responsibility, not a broad generality.

> *McGraw-Hill K-12 Education*, 2000–2020
> * Regional Sales Manager with six direct reports covering fifteen Midwest Sates, 2014–2020.
> * District Sales Manager with three direct reports covering Illinois, Wisconsin, and Indiana, 2007–2013.
> * Sales Representative covering Wisconsin and Illinois, 2000–2006.

While you were in college, you may have had a number of part-time positions related to the specific job for which you are applying. For example, if you are applying for a technology position and in college you designed websites for local small businesses, this should be included under work experience. It indicates that your passion for using technology is more than a passing fancy. In addition, it tells the hiring authority, like the technology director, that you have an interest and aptitude for work in technology.

Awards, Recognition, Community Service

This is a section not often found on resumes, but I encourage its inclusion based on my experience with hiring managers. I have noted that one of the first things that a hiring manger will notice when scanning a resume is a major heading listing awards and recognition for outstanding achievement.

What do you include? Awards for performance from previous employers, like "Employee of the Year Award." Also, go back to your college years and list notable achievements like making the Dean's List or graduating *cum laude.*

Another noteworthy item is your outreach experience, because many employers are community conscious. Hiring managers and human resources directors will give you a big plus mark for your give-back to those in need. Many small businesses and large corporations like Starbucks, Microsoft, Bank of America, and General Electric are community conscious and encourage their employees to participate in outreach efforts.

Technology Skills

In today's world, employers assume that candidates have the technology skills required to be productive workers. However, hiring managers have been burned many times because of this false assumption. If your tech skills are outdated, take an online course from HigherNext or another online organization as verifiable proof to a hiring manager that you are up to speed. Also, you can find technology courses at universities, local community colleges, and online.

No matter what the job or industry, you will be required to use technology to meet your job requirements.

Education

This is the last major heading on your resume and it is very straightforward. Chronologically list college and military (if applicable) education. Also, if you attended a prestigious college prep high school, list that too. Include other professional development courses and certifications. This is how your education section might look.

- The Lawrenceville College Prep High School, Lawrenceville, NJ. Diploma. 1995.
- Elon University, BA. Major: Events Management. Minor: Communications. 2000.
- Elon University Study Abroad. Art History Program. Florence, Italy. 1999.
- The International Culinary Center, New York City. Graduate-level courses in Pastry Arts and Cake Design. 2001.
- Strayer University, Completion of online Web Design course. 2006.
- HigherNext, Online Certified Business Laureate Degree. 2019.

If you authored books or published articles, add a new major heading titled "Publications." Chronologically list all publications in bullet-point format.

Don't add anything after the "Education" section (such as references, favorite sports, ethnicity, gender, religion, or age). If pertinent, you can address these topics during your interview with the hiring manager or human resources director.

WRITING A DIGITAL PROFILE

Always write a digital profile for media such as LinkedIn. It is an important tool that hiring managers, human resources directors, and recruiters use to verify what is on your resume and to read references from colleagues or customers. Therefore, it is important to make sure that your resume and digital profile are in sync. Write your resume first and then create your digital profile.

The digital profile need not be a verbatim repeat of your resume. Extract the most important features of your resume and place them in the appropriate place on the digital profile.

COVER LETTERS

When you send your resume to a named person, always include a one-page cover letter. The cover letter is a summary of your candidacy and explains why you are interested in that particular job and company. It is a business document so format it as such. Include the following five items in your cover letter:

1. Your source of information for the position. Include the name of the person who referred you if applicable.
2. The reason for submitting your resume.
3. A compliment about the company.
4. A brief statement of your background and experience and how it relates to the job description.
5. A post script (PS) suggesting the next step, like scheduling a date for a personal interview.

If you are submitting your resume by email, make the cover letter a part of the email text and attach the resume. If submitting your resume by FedEx or UPS, include a formal typed cover letter rather than a handwritten note on a plain sheet of paper.

MOVING FORWARD

Crafting a resume and digital profile in keeping with today's style is necessary to move your candidacy to the next step, a personal interview with the hiring manager. Where and how to find these decision makers and the companies they represent is key. You will learn all of this in the following chapters.

CHAPTER TAKEAWAYS

- Your digital profile and resume must be in sync. One must reflect the other.
- Spelling and grammar mistakes on your resume will end your chances for employment.
- Today's employers are community conscious. List all outreach activities on your resume.
- Always list awards and special recognitions from past employers, schools, colleges, and civic organizations.

PRINT AND DIGITAL RESOURCES

Career Confidential. www.careerconfidential.com.

Higher Next/Proctor U. www.highernext.com.

Chapter 11

HOW TO FIND DECISION MAKERS AND HIRING MANAGERS

The most serious mistake a mid-career worker can make in the job-hunting process is to believe that writing a "dynamite" resume and emailing it to multiple job boards and career pages is the best way to find a job. What chance do you have when the average medium-sized company receives more than two thousand resumes each month? Who is going to see your resume at Google when the company receives an estimated twenty thousand per day? When you send your resume to Southwest Airlines, it is just one of ninety-eight thousand received each year. Writing a resume is just one step in the job-hunting process. Submitting it to hiring managers and human resources directors is another step, but the process does not stop there. There are additional steps in the process for mid-career workers that I call the Big Ten.

> **The BIG TEN Steps in the Job-Hunting Process**
> 1. Learn who you are and the role you want to play in your new career.
> 2. Find employers in your chosen industry.
> 3. Craft a resume reflecting your new career goals and updated skills.
> 4. Learn what jobs are available with employers you have identified.

5. Find the name of the hiring manager and human resources director for a specific employer and connect personally.
6. Activate your industry and personal networks.
7. Attend trade shows and job fairs.
8. Conduct a successful phone or Skype interview.
9. Conduct a successful personal interview.
10. Negotiate a job offer.

THE PROCESS FOR FINDING DECISION MAKERS

Mid-career workers can fall into complacency when it comes to job hunting. A common error is believing that time in the workplace and a network of contacts will make the process a no-brainer. Making a few phone calls to colleagues and sending out a dozen or so resumes will result magically in finding job opportunities and job offers. Nothing could be more delusional. Employers do not come looking for you at home while you are sitting at your computer sending resumes to job boards and career pages. You must seek them out yourself. If this sounds like a daunting task, fear not, because there are certain tried and true methods for finding employers.

The people you need to contact personally are hiring managers and human resources directors. These are the people in large companies or small businesses who decide who is hired and who is not. If you are seeking a job in sales, the person you need to reach is the sales manager. If you are pursuing a marketing job, the person you should see is the marketing director. If technology is your focus, the person you need to see is the chief technology officer (CTO), or chief information officer (CIO). If you are seeking a position in finance, the person you need to reach is the chief financial officer, the CFO. If you are not sure what role you would like and are seeking opportunities generally, the person you need to see is the human resources director.

Sometimes people at the highest departmental rank will refer you to a subordinate who evaluates all new hires, regardless of rank. See the person to whom you are referred and do not consider this a put down. Be assured that the department head approves all workers hired at any level. For most positions, the first interview is usually with the human resources director who will send the best candidates to the hiring manager who ultimately will make the final decision.

How do you go about finding the people who have the authority to hire you? How do you learn their names and contact information? You may have had the disappointing experience of calling a company and asking for the director of sales only to have the receptionist tell you that all job applicants must go through the human resources department. When that happens, take it to the next level and ask for the name and contact information of the human resources director.

How to Find the Names of Hiring Managers

You can learn the name and contact information for the human resources director, a department head, or hiring manager using these proven methods.

Strategies for Learning the Names of Hiring Managers

- Google the company and the department head's title; e.g., "VP Sales for Walmart."
- Review the company website for the names of its key staff members.
- Network with friends, neighbors, and relatives who are employed.
- Call the company customer service department and ask for the name of the hiring manager.
- Use LinkedIn by entering the name of a company and a position.
- Leave the house and attend conferences and trade shows that take place almost every day in most large- and medium-sized cities across the country.
- Make cold calls at companies located in office and industrial parks.
- Use "old fashioned" methods like the Yellow Pages and newspapers when seeking employment opportunities with local or neighborhood businesses.

PROACTIVE JOB HUNTER

People with the authority to hire you are lurking everywhere. You can find them in airports, on airplanes, in restaurants, bars, Starbucks, sports events . . . any location where people gather. However, just being in a crowd is not enough; you must be proactive.

Finding Hiring Managers at Restaurants and Coffee Houses

When you're at Starbucks ordering a grande cappuccino, most likely the first thing you will do is look for a table that is unoccupied so you can whip out your smartphone or iPad and begin texting or scrolling through the news. This is not the way to find your potential boss. Select a table occupied by those dressed in business attire because they are the people you want to know. Instead of tweeting your life away, begin a conversation with the woman who is dressed for success and pounding away on her laptop. How do you begin the conversation? Begin with that all-time favorite, the weather. "It's really hot out today. Good thing this place has air-conditioning. By the way, you look like the president of a company. What do you do?" Another tactic is to make a comment about Starbucks's successful business model and its college scholarship program for employees. You have just opened the door and who knows what is inside.

One never knows the status of the person in business attire, but it's your job to find out. Contrary to hype, the world of work has not gone entirely casual. Business executives who are on the job customarily dress in business attire. Even in the technology world, executive-level people are dressed a cut above the people working in the trenches. Look for the people in business attire and you will find hiring managers.

Looking for Employers and Hiring Managers in the Yellow Pages

Another way to find employers and their hiring managers may shock you. It is using the Yellow Pages, particularly for jobs with small businesses in your local area. Prior to 1990, people used print books to find just about everything, including employers. One of the most useful books was the Yellow Pages phone directory. It is still being published for every location in the United States, and it is a fascinating book to review. The Yellow Pages are online, too.

The Yellow Pages for a large city like Chicago, Dallas, or New York City can run over a thousand pages. It lists all businesses alphabetically under industry headings. For example, I just clicked on www.yellowpages.com and then entered "insurance companies in New York." The result? Hundreds of companies by name with detailed contact information. For example, I selected Aflac and went to their website and clicked on "Management Team." There I found the name, title, and picture for every key executive including the CEO, marketing director, human resources director, CIO, CTO, and so on down the line. If I were looking for a marketing job with Aflac, I would send my resume and cover letter directly to the named marketing director.

Could anything sounding so *yesterday* really help you find a job in today's digital world? According to Richard Bolles, author of the bestselling job-hunting book *What Color Is Your Parachute?*, workers who use the Yellow Pages to identify potential employers and find the names of hiring managers have a success rate exceeding 50 percent.

You can use either the print or the digital editions. If you know the industry you want to explore just go to that major heading and you will find many companies. Finance. Education. Banking. Publishing. Retailing. Agriculture. Automobiles. Insurance. Healthcare. It's all there . . . in the Yellow Pages.

Back to the Future . . . Again. Using Newspapers to Find Employers

Reading the print or the digital versions of local, regional, or national newspapers is still a productive way to find potential employers and the names of their key personnel. One of the best newspapers to source is the *Wall Street Journal*. I call this daily newspaper America's most honest publication because its agenda makes no bones about its purpose—helping people make money.

Newspapers like the *Wall Street Journal*, the *New York Times*, the *Washington Post*, the *Chicago Tribune*, and the *Los Angeles Times* carry ads for workers at the managerial, director, and vice-president levels, the sweet spots for mid-career workers. Employers spend serious money to advertise these job openings, so you will rarely find ads for entry-level positions. Both print and online weekend editions carry the job ads for mid-level workers and listings of businesses for sale. Be sure to check them out regularly.

Networking

The primary purpose of networking is to connect personally with someone who can help you secure a job. Who are these people? Everyone who is presently employed by a company or who owns a business is a networking source. Where do you find them? They are as close as your next-door neighbor or a former boss. These individuals can direct you to a named person with a job title in their own place of employment.

Your Former Boss

Contact all former bosses and seek their help. Ask for the names of hiring managers at their present employers, and in other companies. Bosses usually know other bosses. Also, you might ask that person for a letter of recommendation. Do not overlook this obvious source. Most people are willing to help let-go workers in their job searches.

Using the Cold-Calling Process to Find Hiring Managers

Mid-career workers who have been out of the job-hunting loop for a number of years tend to forget about protocols, like befriending workers in support positions. You need to be mindful of the importance of workers like receptionists and administrative assistants, "gatekeepers," who control access to the people you want to see. There are gatekeepers in every company, one of the most important being the receptionist at the front desk. When cold calling, the receptionist is the first person you will meet. These individuals can make or break you, and you must treat them with respect and build a relationship quickly. Your appearance and introductory remarks are critical. The receptionist will dismiss anyone who disregards basic business protocols.

The process begins when you enter an office without an appointment. You tell the receptionist that you are seeking a job and would

like to meet with the human resources director or hiring manager
for a specific department. If you are focusing on a specific position,
maybe associate marketing manager, ask to see the hiring manager in
charge of marketing. If you are seeking a position in sales, ask for the
sales manager. Your introductory statement to the receptionist, accompanied with a smile, might go something like this: "Good morning, Ms. Jones. My name is William Foster. I'm seeking a position in
information technology. May I please speak with your technology
director?" The receptionist will respond in one of several ways:

1. "Our technology director is Mrs. Deborah George, and I'll
    see if she's available." Your response might be, "Thank you.
    I would appreciate only a few minutes of her time. I know
    she's a busy person."
2. "Our technology director is Mr. Adams, but he's out of the
    office today." Your response might be, "Thank you. In that
    case, may I speak with his administrative assistant to make
    an appointment to see Mr. Adams?"
3. "We do not have a technology director." Your response
    might be, "Thank you. In that case, may I speak with the
    human resources director?"
4. "I'm sorry, you need an appointment to see any of our staff
    members." Your response might be, "Thank you. May I
    please have the name of your human resources director
    and the email address and phone number? I'll call for an
    appointment as you suggested."

Note that your response should always begin with a "thank you."
Also, note that you never just say "thank you" and walk out. That is
not the way it works in the business world, because the company is
always looking for new talent, like you. Be professionally assertive,
but courteous, until you get what you want and need.

Cold Calls Are Always in Style
Some consider making personal calls on potential employers without
an appointment something out of yesterday's playbook. Wrong! The

purpose of the cold call is not to be hired on the spot; its purpose is to arrange a personal meeting with a hiring manager.

Cold calling is not easy at first, but the more calls you make, the easier it will become. Of course, you risk rejection when you make a cold call. Do not take it personally. Over time, your technique will improve and you will learn that rejection is not a personal insult but part of the business process.

The odds of something happening are in your favor, as the numbers will show. Assume that you make fifteen cold calls per week on potential employers in an industrial or office park. At the end of one month, you will have made sixty calls where you spoke with a real person.

Assuming a success rate of only 10 percent, at the end of one month you will have met personally with six influential people. Compare that to the number of personal interviews you will have had if you stayed at home and fired off resumes to unknown entities.

Working with Executive Recruiters

Another productive way to reach employers is to connect with recruiters. These are individuals who work alone or in partnership, or who are employed by large national or multinational search firms. They are located in every part of the country and abroad.

Most recruiters specialize in a particular industry and job level. For example, recruiters who work for the multinational search firm Heidrick & Struggles, which is based in Chicago, specialize in managerial-level jobs and up. The firm has been successful conducting searches for C-level executives with companies like Coca-Cola. It is one of the giants in the industry and is listed on the New York Stock Exchange. It has offices in every major US city and in many cities abroad as well. Another multinational search firm is Los Angeles–based Korn Ferry. It specializes in C-level and mid-level searches. Both of these search firms have sterling reputations among both employees and customers. Both undertake searches for mid-career managerial candidates for multiple industries.

Individual recruiters and boutique search firms employing several recruiters specialize in a particular industry. Some conduct searches for only one level of employment, like entry level or mid-level. Some work only local job searches and others work nationally or internationally. In addition, some conduct searches only for contract workers, such as computer programmers, who are employed for a stipulated period of time, say twenty-four months.

Recruiters work for employers, not job candidates. They conduct searches for candidates like you, the mid-career worker, to fill a specific job identified by an employer, which could be a small business or a large publicly traded company. Usually the employer pays a fee to the recruiter based on the job's base salary. Most career recruiters work on retainer, which means they are paid a fee in specified increments by the company even if the search is not successful, an infrequent occurrence. Other recruiters work on a contingency basis. They earn a fee only if they provide a candidate who is hired by the company. Recruiters never ask a job candidate for a fee.

Even though recruiters are paid by the employer, their success derives from presenting qualified candidates to the company. Job candidates, like the laid-off mid-career worker looking for new opportunities, are in effect their "products." They want and need job seekers like you to maintain their businesses. They find candidates through networking, attending trade shows, and by using social media such as LinkedIn.

How to Contact a Recruiter
Mid-career workers in a particular industry can find a recruiter by accessing their industry network or by using the Internet. If using the latter method, go online and enter your location, your industry, and job level. For example, Google "Regional sales manager recruiters in St. Louis" or "Recruiters for trade publishing editors in New York." Always enter the industry and the job title. Another tactic is to use LinkedIn. Enter "executive recruiters" and add your industry or job specialty.

To connect with a recruiter in one of the large multinational firms like Heidrick & Struggles, call the company and ask to speak with a recruiter specializing in mid-level jobs in a particular industry.

Procedures for Working with Recruiters

Consider the recruiter a friend who is working for you. Tell her or him how and why you have been laid off or fired and what kind of new opportunities you are seeking. Do not hesitate to disclose your compensation history and what you would like going forward. Recruiters are the best source you can find for information about compensation levels and qualifications because they are in touch with the workplace every day.

The recruiter will ask for your resume. Prepare it using the rubrics in this book and always ask for advice to enhance your resume. For phone, Skype, or personal interviews, follow the advice in this book. Just as you would when working with a potential employer directly, make every effort to meet the recruiter personally. After the vetting process, the recruiters will submit your candidacy for a particular job with a particular company. They will do that by sending your resume and a written review of your interview and qualifications to the company's human resources director or directly to the hiring manager.

Your relationship with the recruiter should be based on honesty and trust. The recruiter is one of your best sources for finding new opportunities. Make every effort to contact a recruiter in your selected industry as soon as you have prepared a viable resume.

MOVING FORWARD

This chapter reviewed *how* to find decision makers and hiring managers using tried and true methods. There is another important step for reaching the Promised Land—learning *where* to find potential employers. In the next chapter, I'll tell you how this is done. Stick with us.

CHAPTER TAKEAWAYS

- Treat the gatekeepers with respect.
- Meeting hiring managers personally is a key step in the process.
- Cold calling on companies in office and industrial parks is an effective strategy to find hiring managers.

PRINT AND DIGITAL RESOURCES

"Job Search Strategies." Lynda.com. www.lynda.com/Business-Skills-tutorials/Job-Search-Strategies/97580-2.html.

Sandberg, Sheryl. *Lean In: Women, Work and the Will to Lead.* Knopf, 2013.

Standard & Poor's 500 Guide 2013: America's Most Watched Companies. McGraw-Hill, 2013.

Chapter 12

WHERE TO FIND EMPLOYERS

Finding employers in your chosen area of the workplace is a task that will prove interesting and successful if you use tried and true strategies. Two of these are using digital technology, which you can do from home, and the other is tearing yourself away from home to attend trade shows, conferences, and job fairs.

GOING ONLINE TO FIND EMPLOYERS

Using online resources creatively can yield positive results, but it is necessary to proceed with caution because online job hunting can steal your time like nothing else. Studies show that using digital media is the least effective way to find employment with one exception—LinkedIn.

USING JOB BOARDS

Job boards have yielded disappointing results for many job hunters. My assessment of the boards is that most fail to connect you with a named person, a hiring authority, and in many cases, even with a named company like Microsoft, Raytheon, or McDonald's.

REVIEWING CORPORATE WEBSITES

To learn what's happening at consumer goods companies, like Procter & Gamble, review their websites and check out their career pages. However, do not assume that all available jobs are posted on company websites. Many jobs, from entry level to mid-level to executive level, go to job boards and recruiters.

When you do respond to a company career page listing, make sure that you respond to a named person with a title. Sending it to "Employment Manager" is a waste of time. The most expedient way to find the name and title of that person is to call the company customer service department and ask for help.

FINDING EMPLOYERS AT OFFICE AND INDUSTRIAL PARKS

In every metropolitan area, you will find office, business, and industrial parks, places where hundreds of companies locate their local offices, regional offices, or home offices. Some parks specialize in one particular industry while others host companies from different industries. For example, an industrial park in Langhorne, Pennsylvania, specializes in medical offices for both physicians and dentists. An industrial park in Portland, Maine, hosts a diversified group of companies including J. Weston Walch Publishing Company, a ninety-year-old educational publisher.

How do you contact companies in a business or industrial park? Easy. You leave the house at 8:00 a.m. in your business attire and armed with business cards and a dozen resumes to distribute to hiring managers and human resources directors. You go from door to door and request a personal meeting with the hiring manager in charge of your field of interest.

One might ask," Do I make a cold call on every business in the business park?" If you are job hunting for any kind of job regardless of industry the answer is *yes*. If you are interested only in positions with insurance companies as an underwriter, sales representative, or claims adjuster, narrow your cold calls to insurance companies. You learn where these companies are by reviewing the online directories for that particular business or office park.

Use the Internet to Find Business Parks

There are many business, office, and industrial parks in every area of the country, and the best way to learn where they are is to Google an entry like, "business parks in Denver, Colorado." I did just that and found the Denver Tech Center, an area along the I-25 corridor southeast of Denver. This business park is home to more than sixty companies spanning a number of industries. The list includes Agilent Technologies, Boeing, Cargill, Centex Homes, JP Morgan, Kodiak Petroleum, Morgan Stanley, Nissan Motor Corp., Time Warner Cable, and Western Union. These are either home offices or regional offices and are potential employers. If you live in the Denver Metro Area, start cold calling at the companies located at the Denver Tech Center.

Here is another example of what you will find. I searched for "industrial parks in Houston, Texas" and found the Beltway Industrial Park, where light manufacturing companies are located. Industrial parks in other locations host large manufacturers as well as warehouses and regional offices. If manufacturing is your thing, you can't go wrong by cold calling on companies in an industrial park dedicated to manufacturers.

To see what is available in the Pacific Northwest I Googled "Seattle business parks" and found enough potential employers, and their locations, to keep me busy job hunting for the next six months.

No matter where you live in the US, you will find office parks and industrial parks located near your home. Does it get any easier?

FINDING EMPLOYERS AT JOB FAIRS

There is a mistaken notion that job fairs are only for entry-level workers. In fact, companies in certain industries conduct job fairs whenever they have a critical need for experienced workers who have managerial talent. For example, financial companies and technology companies need hundreds or even thousands of workers when they develop new products, and one way to attract potential candidates is to conduct a job fair. Go online to learn the date and location of a job fair in your location or your area of interest and expertise. Mid-career workers have an excellent chance to connect because of the experience and expertise they can offer. Laid-off workers have another advantage—they can start work immediately. Attending job fairs is an excellent way to meet potential employers and their hiring managers. There are hundreds available throughout the year at a location within driving distance from your home.

The managers you will meet have one thing in mind—to find the best candidates for job openings. It is all business, so you must go prepared, just as you would for attending a trade show. That means bringing a dozen resumes and calling cards, and dressing appropriately. How you dress could take you to the top of the heap or put you in the trash can.

FINDING EMPLOYERS AT CONFERENCES AND TRADE SHOWS

The best places to find potential employers, in the flesh, are convention centers where conferences and trade shows are held. Here you will find a multitude of potential employers, all under one roof. Attending conferences at major convention centers like McCormick Place in Chicago or the Javits Center in New York City is the best use of your job-hunting time. I know from firsthand experience that many candidates have met their potential employers on the floor of a convention center; in fact, candidates have even been hired on the floor. You will not find a better way to make productive use of your job-hunting time and effort.

What is a Trade Show?

A trade show is a gathering of workers representing companies in a specific industry. The purpose of a trade show is to give companies an opportunity to display their products and advertise their services in exhibit booths located on the floor of a convention center.

Trade shows go by different names—conventions, conferences, exhibits, expos, trade fairs, or trade exhibitions. All mean the same thing. Usually they are held at convention centers, which are located in large cities or state capitals, but occasionally they meet in hotels or resorts that have large rooms for hosting exhibit booths and smaller rooms to host "breakout sessions," where industry experts present new products or discuss research and industry trends.

Industry professional organizations sponsor these shows, which can be very costly. Some of those costs are defrayed by member dues and by conference attendance fees. An example of a trade show is the world's largest technology show called the Consumer Electronics Show (CES), which convenes every January in Las Vegas. In 2017, attendance at this show exceeded one hundred and fifty thousand, including thirty-five thousand people from foreign countries. More than three thousand companies attended and hosted exhibits. Can you imagine three thousand potential employers under one roof? If you are interested in technology, you cannot afford to miss CES.

For those let-go workers who were office-bound and did not attend trade shows, here is another example of what to expect at a trade show hosted at a major convention center. Book Expo America (BEA) is the largest trade show in America for the book publishing industry. BEA held its 2017 annual convention at the Javits Convention Center in New York City. More than twelve hundred companies hosted exhibits on the conference center floor, all staffed by publishing company employees. Some held editorial positions, some were marketing managers, some came from sales, others from finance, and still others from information technology. Where in the world could you find so many potential employers and hiring managers under one roof?

Attending trade shows is the most productive strategy for job hunting. However, what do you do once you are in the convention hall? Once again, attending a trade show is a process.

Preparation Checklist for Attending a Trade Show

One does not just show up at an exhibit and expect miracles to happen. In order to reap maximum benefits, plan for it in advance. Here is a checklist and suggestions for planning purposes.

- Your primary purpose for attending these events is to visit the many exhibit booths where you will find hiring managers. Many shows hold exhibits only on specific days and at specific hours. For example, the dates listed for CES, the technology conference in Las Vegas, may be January 10–16, but the exhibits could be open only on January 11–15, from 10:00 a.m. to 6:00 p.m. You can find this information online, or by calling the conference center or the organization hosting the show. This is important because you are attending the conference primarily to visit the exhibit booths where you will find the hiring managers. There is no need to attend the conference on days when the exhibits are not open.

- The organization sponsoring the conference publishes a list of exhibiting companies in the printed conference program. Frequently the directory will include the names of the representatives who will be attending along with their contact information. Obtain this list either online or at the conference center because it will provide the names and contact information for key executives and hiring managers.

- Bring at least one hundred business cards and twenty resumes to the show each day. The exchange of business cards is still the accepted way to build your list of networking contacts. The resumes are for hiring managers you will meet in the exhibit booths or on the convention center floor.

- When you enter the conference center to attend the show, first go to the registration desk to pay the exhibit fee, obtain your name tag, and pick up the conference program, which is usually tucked in a tote bag. Make sure you get the conference program. Always wear your name tag while in the convention center.

- Almost all shows charge a fee for attendance. Many large trade shows, which are open to the public, charge very low admission fees, in the $25 to $50 range. Fees may vary with the number of days you will attend, your affiliation, and your work status. As an example of fees to attend specialized conferences, a technology education industry trade show called EdNET charges up to $900 for admission, but the fee is worth it. The reason is that six hundred hiring authorities attend this annual convention, including CEOs, presidents, vice presidents for sales, marketing, and product development, chief technology and information officers, and human resources directors. During this three-day conference, you will meet keynote speakers and participate in breakout sessions. Also, you will have an opportunity to present your candidacy for two minutes in front of six hundred hiring authorities. It does not get better than that. Negotiate the lowest entrance fee for this and every conference. Always ask for discounts when you register.

- If you are coming from a distance and plan to stay overnight near the conference center, make hotel reservations well in advance. If the conference center is in a large city like Los Angeles, local hotel rates will be quite steep. Find a hotel or motel just out of town at a more reasonable room rate and then drive to the conference center each day. In addition, some conference organizations negotiate lower room rates with hotels and motels in the area, so always check this out online several months in advance.

- Dress at trade shows is usually casual, but as a job candidate you should always be dressed as though you were going for an interview. You are there to sell your candidacy, and you should dress with that in mind.

What You Do at a Trade Show

Are you ready for a bit of fun? This is where you will have a good time in a very relaxed environment and meet hundreds of full-time company workers, many of whom will be hiring managers. Exhibit halls are crowded with customers who are there to get product information and to visit company representatives. This is a place where workers conduct business in a pleasant way. Workers in the various exhibit booths will be dressed informally, many times wearing a casual shirt or top bearing the name of the company and the company logo. Remember, however, that you are not a worker here and you should be in business attire.

After you register and get your name tag, enter the exhibit hall and begin visiting each booth. You can start your booth visits in the first aisle and proceed around the hall until you have stopped at each booth. If there are hundreds of exhibits, this may take two or even three days.

What Do You Say After You Say "Hello"?

When you enter an exhibit booth, view the products on display and ask one of the representatives to explain what the company does. Establish a personal relationship by learning what the person's job is and how he or she likes working for the company. After you establish the relationship, tell the person you are job hunting and ask to speak with a hiring manager who may be there. If you are interested in marketing and the director of marketing is not there, ask for that person's name and contact information, and follow up with a phone call or email when you return to your home office.

If all of this is new to you, here is a script you might use to break the ice when visiting an exhibit booth. Establish the relationship by addressing the worker by name, which is always on the name tag. Here is a sample script.

Script for Talking with a Company Representative at a Trade Show

"Hello, Tom. My name is Jennifer, and I'm here for two reasons and would appreciate your help. First, I would like to know more about your company and what you do. Second, I'm seeking employment and would like to see the hiring manager for marketing if this person is attending the conference. If not, would you please write his or her name and contact information on the back of your business card for me? Also, could you give me the name and contact information for the company human resources director? Thanks, Tom."

Before you leave the exhibit booth, give your business card to your new contact and write on the back, "Seeking employment and would appreciate your help."

If a hiring manager you want to see is in the booth, request a few minutes for an informal interview and give that person your resume. The way to get this moving without feeling awkward is to say something like this: "Bill, here's my resume and if you have the time now, maybe you could take a minute to review it. I'm looking for a job opportunity in marketing and, being in mid-career, I have a wealth of experience. If you don't have time now, could we make an appointment to chat for a few minutes, maybe over a cup of coffee or lunch? My treat, of course."

Where the Hiring Managers and Recruiters Hang Out

The big guys, the hiring managers, always attend trade shows and conventions in order to meet their key customers, to keep up with industry trends, *and* to recruit workers for all levels of employment. Recruiters, too, often attend these shows to prospect for new clients, to seek workers for open positions, or to look for qualified candidates to place in their database for future reference. I have attended hundreds of conferences to recruit job candidates and seek new clients and have never been disappointed. In the job-hunting world, trade shows and exhibits *are* the Promised Land. Visiting these shows is the best way to search for a new job as you rebuild your career after being fired or laid off.

How to Recognize a Hiring Manager

In exhibit booths and on the convention center floor, you will see people dressed in formal business attire. Often, these are the company executives, the people you need to meet. Lacking an introduction, you just have to wing it. Walk up to that person and say something like this: "I can tell by the way you're dressed that you must be running the show here. My name is John and I'm here job hunting. I'm looking for a sales position. Could you steer me in the right direction? I would really appreciate your help." This person will appreciate your sense of humor and the subtle note of respect and recognition.

Lunch Is a Time for Networking

On the convention center floor, there will be formal restaurants, kiosks selling hot dogs and soft drinks, and sometimes bars selling alcoholic drinks. This is another place to meet people. After you buy a burger and a Coke, find a table that is partially occupied. Take a seat, introduce yourself to the person next to you, and go into your sales pitch. Lunch is not just lunch; it is a networking opportunity. You never select an empty table, whip out your smartphone, and begin texting. Never. Why waste your time and money when you could be meeting potential employers?

Thirsty for a Cold Beer?
Convention center restaurants frequently sell alcoholic drinks. *Never* buy them. Do not even think of it. A cardinal rule is never to drink anything alcoholic while job hunting, even if others around you are. You are here on business, not to throw down a beer or a Malbec. Many of the people here are hiring managers and they could be sizing up your personal habits. Company managers do not hire candidates who drink while job hunting. The same rules apply to using any form of controlled substances.

Finding Jobs with Convention Centers

When you review the conference center website, always check out the career postings. Convention centers, such as the Cobo Center in Detroit, are profit-making organizations and employ many workers across all specialties. These are good full-time jobs in sales, marketing, technology, finance, and human resources. In addition, go to the conference center offices and inquire about job opportunities when you attend the conference.

How to Find a Trade Show Catering to a Particular Interest

There are many sources to find conventions matching your interests: industry journals, both print and digital, local newspapers, and convention center schedules. In addition, you will find a trade show directory on the website of Events in America, (www.eventsinamerica. com/tradeshows). This organization tracks and publicizes the names and locations of industry trade shows across the country.

MOVING FORWARD

Attending trades shows is the best strategy for finding hiring managers in the flesh. Trade shows convene every week in large metropolitan areas. To learn the who, when, and where, search the convention center websites. For a directory of major convention centers and a review of the top convention centers and trades shows refer to appendix A and appendix B of this book. I suggest doing this now, because this information will save you hours of time and lead you to places where you will meet hiring managers.

The next step in the process is the interview, which some consider an intimidating event. In the next chapter, I'll provide guidelines for navigating your interview.

CHAPTER TAKEAWAYS
- The best place to meet hiring managers and key executives is at conferences, trade shows, and job fairs.
- Access the convention center website for a list of upcoming trade shows.
- Dress in business attire while attending trade shows.

PRINT AND DIGITAL RESOURCES
Events in America. www.eventsinamerica.com/tradeshows.

The appendices of this book. Here you will find a list of major convention centers by state and the names of important trade shows by industry.

Chapter 13

INTERVIEW RUBRICS FOR MID-CAREER WORKERS

Millions of words have been written about interviews. For example, Google "job interviews," and you will get thousands of hits. Go to the business and career sections at a Barnes & Noble bookstore, and you will find dozens of books on interviews. All of us have read Internet hits titled "Ten tips for killer interviews," or "Ace the interview in three easy steps," or "Interviews for dummies." All of this tells us that the interview is an important part of the job-hunting process and that we should prepare for it carefully.

THE PURPOSE OF THE INTERVIEW

Before we get into the heart of the interview process, let's reconstruct the bigger picture. The interview is a part of the process that enables both you and the company to determine if the relationship will work to the advantage of both the company and the candidate. When that happens, everyone wins. The company makes money from your productive work in order to pay your salary and benefits, expenses, taxes, and perhaps contribute to charitable causes, and still have enough left over to be a profitable business. You win because you make money to become self-sufficient, take care of your family, and give back money and time to the community.

WHO'S HOLDING THE ACES?

Even though the interviewer appears to hold all of the cards, it really is not so. The hiring manager needs someone like you to fill an important position and is under pressure to find the right candidate as soon as possible.

While the hiring manager is evaluating the person across the desk, smart candidates are sizing up the hiring manager as well. It is important that the hiring manager is someone you respect, someone who shows courtesy and honesty. If you find that the interviewer lacks these qualities, erase that company from your list. You may need a job, but you do not want it at the expense of working on a ship of fools. If, for some reason, you think that this listing ship might change once the company hires you, remember this rule: *you can't fix crazy!*

LISTEN AND LEARN

All candidates, especially mid-career workers, want to tout their accomplishments and general work experience to anyone who will listen. They tend to smother the interviewer with a recitation of what's on the resume. The interviewer has most likely checked out who you are and what you have done and is not interested in your retelling it. The person sitting across the desk from you is forward-looking. Keep that in mind when the interviewer begins the conversation by asking questions. Listen and comprehend, because it is how you respond that really counts.

In his well-known book, *The Seven Habits of Highly Effective People*, Stephen Covey says, "Most people do not listen with the intent to understand; they listen with the intent to reply. They are either speaking or preparing to speak."

A good example that supports Covey's theory is the TV interview. Interviewers are often more concerned with presenting their own agendas than with listening for responses to questions they ask. Why don't they permit the person to complete the answer? Before the response is even completed, the interviewer interrupts with her own statement.

Your interviewer, too, might have the same tendency, so be sure to maintain the integrity of the interview to make your point. If the interviewer interrupts before you have the last word out of your mouth, you need to make an appropriate response to keep the interview on an even keel, even though your gut reaction might be, "Shut up. Let me finish my answer to your question."

Here is what you might say when this happens: "To complete my response to your first question, here is what I was going to say . . ." That should keep the interview on the right track and make for a fruitful exchange of ideas and courteous discourse.

The interview is a conversation where two people listen, comprehend, and then respond. There are two basic rules for interviews.

> **The Two Golden Rules for Interviews**
> 1. Be courteous.
> 2. Be honest.

These two rules build the foundation for all personal relationships. This holds true no matter how young, how old, or how senior the interviewer is. And it applies if you have been laid off or fired from your last job. If the interviewer asks you why you left your previous job, be honest and say that you were let go. If you were laid off, state the circumstances: a reorganization, downsizing, rightsizing, or bankruptcy. If you were fired, don't talk around it. Be forthcoming and state why you were fired: that you did not meet the job expectations, or that you and your boss were on different pages. Admit it and follow by saying that you have learned your lesson and that you have resolved to move forward using your newfound persona and your reconstructed character. (As a matter of fact, the interviewer most likely learned that you had been fired for cause after some preliminary background checking before you came for the interview, so do not try to hide it.)

THE INTERVIEWER'S AGE AND RANK

The person sitting across the desk from you may be older than you are and may be at the director or vice president level. To reach that point in the corporate hierarchy, this person has been doing something right.

On the other side of the age situation, the interviewer may be ten years your junior and display arrogance that is nothing short of irritating. Suck it up, because you cannot do anything about it. Build the relationship by expressing interest in this person's rise to a position of responsibility.

Regardless of the situation, the only way to deal with these variables is to be prepared to answer the questions in a mature manner and on your own terms. When you prepare for the interview, resolve that you are going to look at the hiring manager as a potential friend.

HOW THE INTERVIEWER JUDGES YOU

Three important items on an employer's checklist appear so self-evident that candidates overlook them. However, if you fall short on any of the three, your chances of moving ahead in the process are diminished.

Appropriate Dress

Your appearance is the first thing a hiring manager notices. If you come to an interview dressed inappropriately, you are history. Case closed. No second chance. With the workplace becoming more casual, there is a tendency to dress down, even for an interview. We see mid-level and executive-level workers in casual dress when on the job, but an interview is a different occasion. I have asked human resources directors about this, and their advice is to dress a cut above casual for an interview. In fact, several told me that many experienced candidates, mid-level and executive level, dress too casually for interviews and it does not help their candidacy. Their advice is to wear business attire for an interview.

Appropriate Language

After dress, the most important checklist item is verbal communication, which includes vocabulary. Avoid clichés and slang terms. Answer questions using business-speak that you have learned throughout your working years. The hiring manager expects no less. For example, one of the question most frequently asked is "Why do you want to work here?" Deliver your answer in business language such as this:

> *I want to work with your company because I'm impressed with your record of generating revenue. For example, in the last quarter your revenue was up 10 percent over a comparable quarter a year ago. This tells me that you have a viable business model. I would like a chance to work for such a company and contribute my time and talents to help the company continue to grow.*

Appropriate Body Language

There are two parts to the interview; what you say and how you say it—content and delivery. The content part of the interview should reflect your research on the company's finances, your interest in the job opportunity at hand, and your qualifications for helping the company move forward. The delivery part of your conversation includes the unspoken word—body language—which reflects your level of confidence and your interest in the job and company.

Many words have been written on this subject, but it still comes down to a few basics. Sit straight, make eye contact, relax, smile, and display your personality. If you are not accustomed to using your hands to make a point, do not make an awkward attempt to do this in an interview. You are having a conversation about how you can help the company going forward, not auditioning for a part in a movie. To learn more on this general topic, conduct a Google search on body language.

Here is a real-life situation that I encountered recently while conducting a search for a vice president. This story demonstrates that delivery, particularly the body language part of it, is just as important as content.

Fred from California

Fred had a personal two-hour interview with the CEO of a major company located in Los Angeles. The position, vice president for international sales and marketing, required the candidate to live in the home office area, and Fred met that requirement. He did not need to relocate. This was a huge problem out of the way. On paper, he met every job requirement and more. So far, so good. However, something untoward happened during the interview process. The CEO rejected his candidacy citing these two reasons. One, "Fred's answers seemed shallow." In other words, the CEO did not buy the content. Two, "Fred appeared insecure, lacking confidence, and appeared to be distracted." His body language told the CEO that there was a disconnect. His eyes were wandering during the interview, his posture was strained, his arms were folded much of the time, and his legs were crossed during the interview. Fred's body language told the CEO that he was not buying into the conversation.

I counseled Fred on the basics of body language and persuaded the CEO to have a second interview with Fred. Specifically, I told Fred to sit erect facing the interviewer, make direct eye contact throughout the interview, sit with hands resting in his lap rather than folded, rest legs on the floor rather than tightly crossed, and avoid fidgeting and letting eyes wander if there are interruptions from office sources, like a ringing phone. Also, I told Fred to relax and maintain a friendly smile during the interview. The CEO obliged by granting Fred a second interview and the results were startling. The interview proceeded as a conversation, and the CEO and Fred learned they had much in common on a personal level. Both were star performers on their college swim teams and both had similar current interests. After another round of interviews with company executives, Fred was hired.

PREPARING A WRITTEN INTERVIEW AGENDA

I am always impressed when a candidate comes to an interview with a written agenda that includes questions about both the position and the company. I'm equally impressed when the candidate hands me a written agenda and requests a brief discussion of each topic if time permits. A written agenda sends a powerful message that you have carefully prepared for the interview and that you are pursuing *this* particular opportunity, not just any job. Here is a sample agenda that you can use as a model for crafting your own, which you can then print on your letterhead and hand to the interviewer before beginning the interview.

Sample Interview Agenda

Subject: Agenda for Interview with Amazon

Position: Director of Inside Sales

Candidate: Lisa Hopkins

Human Resources Director: Joseph Kowalski

Date: June 7, 2018

I would appreciate the opportunity to discuss the following questions during my interview with Mr. Kowalski:

1. Why is this position open?
2. If someone else had this job, why did that person leave the company?
3. Why are you considering me for this position?
4. Would superior performance in this position lead to a promotion?
5. What are the three major expectations for the Director of Inside Sales?
6. To whom does this job report and what is that person's management style?
7. What is the background of the person to whom this position reports?
8. What is the company's revenue goal for this fiscal year? How much of an increase is that over the previous year's revenue?
9. What has made this company a leader in the industry?
10. Does the company participate in community outreach programs?

11. Does the company require ongoing professional development courses?
12. Why should I join Amazon?

> I thank you for discussing these issues during our interview.
> Sincerely,
> *Lisa*
> Lisa Hopkins

Answers to these questions are a tool for evaluating the position and company. You need this information to determine if you want to continue the process or decline. Using the written interview agenda will separate you from the rest of the pack. Do not hesitate to use this technique for every interview.

THE INTERVIEW PROCESS

The interview process has four sections each with its own set of procedures:

1. The beginning of the interview. This is the introductory phase, which sets the tone for the interview.
2. The body of the interview, which takes place after the greetings are completed.
3. Interviewing the interviewer.
4. The ending of the interview, a critically important action item.

Before each interview, write your plan detailing how you will deal with each section. Let's explore each part in detail.

How the Interview Begins

After you exchange hellos and informal chitchat, like "This is just a beautiful day. I'm happy spring has finally come after such a harsh winter," it is show time.

Trying to anticipate what the interviewer will ask can be a never-ending game. To level the playing field and keep this a true give-and-take rather than an interrogation, plan to incorporate some or all of these five topics into the interview:

- You are here because you have learned there is a specific employment opportunity.
- You have researched the company and would like to work there for several reasons. State what they are. Some reasons could be your interest in their product, company profitability, glowing reports from company workers, or the steady increase in the price of the company stock.
- You would like an opportunity to increase company profitability by using your talents, intelligence, energy, and passion.
- Highlight your successes and awards for achievement. Verbalize the key points on your resume under the major heading "Awards, Recognition, Community Service."
- State your career goals and do not be shy. If you really would like to be the company president someday, say so. Tell your interviewer how and why you believe you could work your way up to that position.

One never knows where an interview will go, and it is really up to the candidate to set the direction and tone of the interview. Your written agenda will help accomplish this. Naturally, the interviewer has a certain number of questions, but you do not know these in advance. However, the interviewer will ask one question in almost every situation: "Would you tell me about yourself?" It appears to be a trivial question, but that's just the way it is, and you have to prepare for it. If you are caught off guard, you might end up reciting your family history or rendering a chronological account of your life from birth to the present. What the hiring manager really wants to hear is what you might do for the company if you are hired, rather than hearing that you like a latte better than a cappuccino.

How do you answer that question? It could go several ways, but here is a script that you might use. It gives direction to the interview and sets the tone for a dialogue instead of a Q&A session.

Script Answer for "Would You Tell Me About Yourself?"
I'm the kind of person who takes responsibility for my own life, and that includes having a position that will give me income to continue to be self-sufficient and accomplish my career goals. I'm here because I believe that your company can provide that opportunity. My research indicates that your last quarter generated revenue that exceeded expectations and that your past three years were profitable. I want to be part of a company with that kind of track record because it means that you are doing something right. I would like to build on that success by applying my intelligence, energy, and passion to make this company even better and more profitable. Also, my career vision includes a vice president–level position and hopefully I can that find that here.

Read this aloud several times until you make it your own. Modify it to include some hard numbers and specifics from your resume.

The Body of the Interview and Frequently Asked Questions
Candidates, understandably, are curious about what the interviewer will ask. The kinds of questions asked in an interview follow a somewhat standard format. Here are questions the interviewer may ask regardless of the company or position.

1. Would you tell me something about yourself?
2. How did you find out about us?
3. Why do you want to work here?
4. What are your major qualifications for this position?
5. Are there any areas where you think you need to improve?
6. What is your career goal?
7. Can you tell me about a work problem you encountered and how you resolved it?

8. What are your compensation requirements?
9. When could you begin work with us if we agree this is the right job for you?
10. Have you participated in community outreach programs?
11. What is your main academic interest?
12. What books have you read recently?
13. Give me an example of how you use social media like YouTube, Twitter, Facebook, and LinkedIn?
14. What do you want to know about the company and the job?
15. Why did you leave your last job?

You don't know how many of these questions the interviewer will ask, but be prepared to answer all of them. Conduct a rehearsal before the interview by having a trusted friend ask you these questions and then deliver your responses. Practice until you feel comfortable with your answers. Remember to quantify as much as possible.

Interviewing the Interviewer
You can begin evaluating the hiring manager by asking a question like, "Could you tell me about your job experience, such as how long you have been here, what your responsibilities are, and what you did before taking this job?"

Such dialogue permits the hiring manager to brag a little and tell you some success stories. Your expressed interest in the hiring manager's accomplishments helps build the relationship and provides valuable information to evaluate this person. In addition, it makes the interview conversational rather than interrogative.

Remember, this is *your* interview and you are entitled to ask as many questions as necessary to learn about the company and its people. Do not be intimidated by the interviewer's status or title. This is your interview, your time, your career, your life.

Questions to Ask the Interviewer
Most likely, you will have your own list of questions, but here are five you should always ask according to Jeff Haden, a very successful executive recruiter and author of many articles and a book on job

hunting and interviewing. This material appeared in his article "Five Questions Job Candidates Should Ask," which appeared in an issue of *INC*. online magazine.

1. *What really drives success for the company?* Every profitable company has rubrics that account for its success. Learn what these are, and you will know much about the company and what it expects from its workers. If you hear something like, "Everyone here works like crazy, even coming in on Saturdays and Sundays," consider it a yellow flag. You should not have to spend seven days a week meeting job expectations, and you should not be expected to be on call via texts and email 24/7, unless you are a medical professional or a law enforcement officer . . . or president of the United States.

2   *What do employees do in their spare time?* This might be a difficult question for the interviewer to answer, especially in a large company. However, the answer will tell you much about the kind of people the company hires, and if these are your kind of people. Do they spend off-work hours at a sports bar? Do they volunteer their off-work hours for company-sponsored outreach programs? Do some of them take graduate-level courses to improve their work skills?

3. *How do you plan to deal with . . . ?* The blank part of this question could be any number of items that aroused your curiosity while doing your research on the company and the industry. The question could be, "How do you plan to deal with lower margins for your technology products?" The answers to these questions will tell you if the company recognizes its problems and how it plans to deal with them going forward.

4. *What do you expect me to accomplish in the first sixty to ninety days?* This question lets the interviewer know that you are no slouch. You want the company hiring manager to know that you are ready, willing, and able to be productive immediately. You are job-ready.

5. *What are the common attributes of your top performers?* The answer to this question will tell you much about the corporate culture, the company expectations, and what workers are willing to do in order to be successful there.

Ending the Interview

There is a definite way to end the interview. Salespeople ask for the order after making their product presentation instead of just saying, "Thank you for your time" and leaving. The same holds true for the interview. Close by saying thank you and, if you are interested in the job and the company, ask, "What are the next steps in the process? I really would like to work here based upon your answers to my questions and my research about the company. When can I start?"

If the interviewer gives a nebulous answer to your closing statements, counter with an action item like, "Thanks for your time. I'll follow up with you by phone or email to check on the status of my candidacy. May I please have your business card? And by the way, what is your hiring deadline?"

If you are not interested in the job, say so and leave after saying, "Thank you for your time. I really do not think this is a good fit. I'm sure that you will find a candidate better suited for this position."

Remember to send a follow-up letter even if you are no longer interested in the job. Always maintain the relationship regardless of the results of the interview.

PANEL INTERVIEWS

Occasionally, a panel instead of just one person will conduct the interview for the company. The panel interview may sound intimidating, but it can work to your advantage.

Panels usually consist of the hiring manager, the company human resources director, and a worker from the department where the job is located. For example, if you are interviewing for an editorial manager position with a publishing company, the worker may be an associate editor.

The purpose of the panel interview is to save time, not to intimidate the candidate. When you walk in the door, you don't know if the interview will be with one person or with a panel, so be prepared mentally for both. Usually a panel interview means that the company is seriously interested in your candidacy. It's a positive sign for you. Be reassured and confident that the interview is going to work to your advantage. After the interview begins, determine the person who appears to be most friendly and supportive and make an effort to build a relationship with him or her.

Interviewing with a panel is advantageous for a number of reasons. In the one-on-one interview, if you do not connect with the person across from you, there is nobody else you can turn to for help. In a panel interview, you have options for building strong relationships with more than one person.

BREAKFAST, LUNCH, OR DINNER INTERVIEWS

Occasionally the hiring manager will invite you to interview over breakfast, lunch, or dinner. The reason is not hunger. Rather, this type of an interview gives the manager an opportunity to observe your behavior in a real-life setting. Candidates for customer-contact jobs in sales or marketing are frequently subjected to interviews over a meal. There are several basic rubrics for such interviews:

- Table manners should be scrupulously observed. That means chewing with your mouth closed, not leaning on the table, and not slurping your soup or coffee.
- Never lick your fingers.
- Never drink alcoholic beverages at meal interviews, even if the interviewer does.
- Never take calls on your smartphone. In fact, turn it off and put in your pocket or purse.
- Treat the wait staff and clean-up crew with respect.
- Remain focused regardless of circumstances.

These may sound like adolescent suggestions, but I have included them because I have observed violations of basic manners on a number of occasions while interviewing mid-career candidates. On one occasion, I was interviewing a candidate for the presidency of a publishing company, and she licked her fingers after finishing her entrée. In effect, she licked her way out of a job. I have interviewed many job candidates over breakfast and lunch. Most observed our rubrics, but a number did not, with devastating results—loss of a job opportunity. Here's just one example that highlights the benefits of adhering to the rules.

Mark the Marine

I was interviewing a candidate over breakfast for a sales manager position at the Marriott Hotel restaurant, located at Liberty International Airport in Newark, New Jersey. It was early morning, crowded, and tables were close together. At the table next to us sat a young couple with a screaming baby who was distracting me to the point where I was ready to ask the host to change our location. However, candidate Mark kept the conversation going as if there were no distractions. He did not even look at the unhappy baby. This caught my attention, and I gained a great deal of respect for Mark because of his discipline and understanding. We proceeded through the interview for ninety minutes and Mark won not only my respect but also my recommendation for the job. When I asked Mark how he kept his cool, he replied, "In the Marines, I learned discipline and how to stay focused in difficult situations."

PHONE AND SKYPE INTERVIEWS

The phone/Skype interview is a standard part of the job-hunting process because of the large number of candidates applying for posted jobs, and because of the distance between candidate and interviewer. When a human resources director has a hundred applicants for one position, he makes the first cut using the candidate's resume and information from other sources like social media. After the list is narrowed to a handful of candidates, the next step is to evaluate them with a phone or Skype interview. The process is sometimes called a "phone screening." Company execs claim the phone and Skype interview process is cost effective.

These interviews usually are not conversations but interrogations leaving candidates with little time to do more than answer rapid-fire questions. The interviewer has a list of questions on her desk and wants to run through them as quickly as possible. It is akin to a robotic procedure. The candidate is rarely given time to ask questions or offer more than a perfunctory answer to questions posed by the interviewer.

Try to avoid the phone screening by volunteering to come in for a personal interview, even if this means driving three hours each way to the company location. Face-to-face communication is what you need to move forward in the search process, and the phone interview gets in the way.

The Purpose of the Phone or Skype Interview

The only purpose of the phone interview is to move your candidacy to the next step, the personal interview with the hiring manager. Nobody is ever hired because of a phone or Skype interview. It's just another step in the process. It permits the interviewer to screen out unqualified candidates and select finalists for personal interviews. It does not seem fair because the hiring manager or human resources director is holding the cards, but that's the way it is. You cannot change some things, so you must learn to live with them and do your best. The phone/Skype interview is one of them.

Phone and Skype Interview Preparation Checklist

Talking on the phone comes naturally to some people, but most of us have a less-than-winning phone personality. However, with adequate preparation anyone can accomplish the mission successfully. Prepare for the interview just as you would for a personal interview using this checklist.

- Find a private location for the interview, preferably your home office where there will be absolute quiet.
- Eliminate traffic noise, barking dogs, crying babies, and music playing in the background. If there are two phones in your location, turn off the one not being used. The last

thing you want is your alternate phone ringing during an interview.

- Avoid holding the interview in casual settings such as a restaurant, car, bar, or train. This is a business call, not a casual call. If there are barking dogs or clinking glasses in the background, surely the interviewer will hear the background noise, and you will be history. There are no second chances.

- Take the call at a table or desk where you can spread out documents for reference. You cannot do this while driving your car.

- Have your resume, the job description, company information, and a written interview agenda listing your questions in front of you during the call. Also, have a tablet or notebook and a pen for note-taking. Handwrite notes instead of entering them on your desktop or laptop computer or smartphone. With today's sensitive audio technology, keyboard noise is distracting to the person on the other end of the line.

- Stay focused. On a separate sheet of paper, write the name of the company, the name and title of the person with whom you will be speaking, the date, time, and location of the interviewer.

- If the interviewer is located in another time zone, make the adjustment. If you are in New York and the interviewer is in Denver, there will be a two-hour time difference, so plan accordingly. If the call is scheduled for 9:00 a.m., Mountain Time, it will be 11:00 a.m. in New York. If you miscalculate the time difference and the caller gets your voicemail instead of your voice, you will be history.

- Take the call dressed in business attire, because the way you dress sets the stage for your behavior. If you are dressed in a yoga outfit, your conversation could easily become too casual. The same applies to your body language. If you take the call with bare feet resting on the top of your desk, you could slip into casual mode and begin using words like "awesome."

- Prepare to answer the question "Would you tell me something about yourself?"

- Select the three most important questions from your written agenda. Usually phone interviews are time sensitive, so you want to make sure you have covered what is important *to you*. If the interviewer permits you to continue, go beyond the first three questions. Phone and Skype interviews, like personal interviews, should be a two-way conversation, which entitles you to be a proactive part of it. Your time is just as valuable as that of the interviewer.
- Have your laptop or desktop computer running with the company website on the screen.
- Smile during the interview. A smile on your face will relax you and make the tone more conversational. Think of the phone smile as virtual body language.
- If you are using a smartphone for the interview, conduct a test run to make sure the connection works.

Navigating the Phone or Skype Interview

Etiquette is everyone's concern. Should you address the interviewer by first or last name? Is it Mrs., Ms., Mr., Dr., or Mary? It is important to get it right. Here are some guidelines that follow the "listen first" rule.

If the interviewer introduces herself as "Mrs. Smith, human resources director," then you address her as Mrs. Smith throughout the interview. If she introduces herself as "Barbara Smith," call her Barbara. Never, under any circumstances, address a person using a nickname like "Barb" if she introduces herself as Barbara.

If the interviewer introduces himself as "Dr. William Ford," call him "Dr. Ford" throughout the interview. If the interviewer introduces himself as "Bob Ford, sales manager," call him Bob. If the interviewer introduces himself as "John Cupcake," call him John, not "Jack." A common error is to assume it is permissible to call a person by a shortened version of his or her name. I have found that the most frequently abused first name is "Robert." Why does everyone revert to "Bob"?

After You Say "Hello"

The first thing to ask after you say hello and make introductory chit-chat is "How much time do we have?" Knowing this will tell you how much time to spend answering questions, and how much time you have for asking questions that are on your interview agenda. Write the end time on a piece of paper and refer to it throughout the conversation. After learning the amount of time you have, tell the interviewer that you have several questions you would like to ask and find out when it would be appropriate to do so. It could be the last thing on the agenda, or the first.

Closing the Phone or Skype Interview

The close is the same for the phone interview and the Skype interview. Learn the interviewer's phone number and email address, say thank you for the interview, and ask for the job. The script for closing all interviews is the same: "Thank you for your time and consideration. What are the next steps in the process? I really would like to work here based on your answers to my questions and my research about your company. When can I start?"

After the interview, follow up by mailing or emailing a thank-you note.

FOLLOW-UP LETTERS

Courtesy dictates that you send a follow-up letter or email to the interviewer(s) after every personal, phone, or Skype interview. This is a business document so format it accordingly. Include the following items:

- A thank you for the opportunity to interview for the position.
- A reaffirmation of your interest in the position and the company.
- A statement asking for the job.
- A post script (PS) after your closing signature. This is an action item such as, "I will call you on Wednesday, March 10, to continue the conversation and answer any questions you might have about my candidacy. What is the best time to call?

Send the follow-up letter by email *and* by FedEx or UPS. I recommend using traditional services because hard copy has a tendency to stay on the recipient's desk. An email doc disappears with a quick click, never to be seen again.

MOVING FORWARD

All types of interviews have one purpose: to see if you and the employer are on the same page for continuing the process. If you believe you are, pursue the job until you get an offer or a definite rejection. Do not let the process hang unresolved.

Mid-career workers come to the interview with a work history and an idea of what they need for compensation. The most frequent objections to one's candidacy are overqualification, compensation requirements that are too high, and lack of certain education requirements. In the next chapter, I'll discuss all of these issues.

CHAPTER TAKEAWAYS
- Build a friendly relationship with the interviewer. Friends hire friends.
- Body language is crucial nonverbal communication.
- Observe basic manners during interviews at restaurants.
- Control the interview process by preparing a written agenda to share with the interviewer.
- Practice reciting answers to possible questions.
- The purpose of the phone or Skype interview is to move your candidacy to the next step, the personal interview.

PRINT AND DIGITAL RESOURCES

"12 Job Interview Tips for Women." www.EducatetoAdvance.com.

Covey, Stephen. *The 7 Habits of Highly Effective People: Powerful Lessons in Personal Courage.* Simon & Schuster, 2013.

Inc. magazine. www.inc.com/author/jeff-haden. Articles by Jeff Haden dealing with the interview process.

Kuhnke, Elizabeth. *Body Language for Dummies.* Wiley, 2012.

Chapter 14

OVERCOMING OBJECTIONS TO YOUR CANDIDACY

Job candidates who have been fired or laid off frequently report that potential employers voice three objections to their candidacy:

1. Sorry! You are overqualified.
2. Sorry! Your compensation requirements are too high.
3. Sorry! You do not have the education requirements for this job.

Sometimes these are unrealistic or perceptual objections. Sometimes they are accurate. Whatever the case, you must be prepared to deal with these three objections during interviews.

SORRY! YOU ARE OVERQUALIFIED

The overqualification objection is usually raised during the personal interview and most candidates never see it coming. They assume that the hiring manger would be delighted to have an experienced candidate who could be productive on day one.

A typical situation finds the candidate, a let-go worker at the director level, interviewing for a job titled "director." It seems to be a lateral move, so the candidate feels confident that this will work. Toward the end of the interview the hiring manager says, "Mary, you have all of the qualifications listed in the job description, and there is no doubt you can do the job. However, you have more experience than we need for this job. In short, I think you are overqualified." This jarring statement leaves you scrambling for a lucid response. Here are possible responses you can offer to the hiring manager when this happens to you.

Responses to the Overqualification Objection

Your first reaction might be disappointment and a gut verbal response and body language that seal your fate: "That's ridiculous. Why should my experience disqualify me? My twenty years in this industry should put me at the top of your list."

Here are some more productive responses that might overcome this objection and keep the conversation moving forward:

- "Thank you for recognizing my background and experience. Moving forward, I think the depth and breadth of my experience would be valuable to your cause. I could help take some of the pressure from your job and make your life easier. Combine your knowledge of the company culture and operations with my depth and breadth of experience, and together we could take this department to a higher level. I think we would make a great team."
- "I understand why you might feel that I'm overqualified, and I'm flattered that you have given that much thought to my candidacy. However, rest assured that I will not use my experience to steamroll your status and authority in the department. I'm not after your job. I'm looking for work-life balance and believe that I can find that here. I think we would make a great team."
- "I might bring more to the table than you need right now, but I assure you that I'm not looking for just another paycheck until I find something better. I've targeted your company for its stability, profitability, and employee-friendly culture. I think we would make a great team."
- "I'm looking for more than a paycheck and job title. And my overqualifications? You could use my experience to your

advantage. In addition, I like you personally, and I think we could make a great team."

- "I can understand why you might feel that way. However, my qualifications, particularly in the technology sphere, could be of value to the company going forward. Technology is moving at lightning speed, and I can help the company keep up with the rest of the pack. In addition, I reviewed your profile on LinkedIn and believe our tech skills are complimentary. I think we would make a great team."

You may have noticed that each one of the responses is positive and includes a statement of working together as a team. When a potential boss is confronted by a candidate whose background, experience, and qualifications exceed hers, the survival instinct kicks in. Unknowingly, she could see you as a competitor for her job. Human beings are in survival mode every waking hour without even realizing it.

The best way to allay fears of the potential boss is to research her background and experience to search for common and complimentary attributes and interests. Articulate that at the beginning of the interview to begin building a friendly relationship. Remember one of the cardinal rules of job hunting: friends hire friends.

SORRY! YOUR COMPENSATION REQUIREMENTS EXCEED OUR BUDGET

Compensation is a serious issue for let-go workers who are job hunting. The expectation is that you should get what you had in your last job, or more. Assume the base salary in your last job, business development manager, was $95,000. Going forward into job-hunting mode that is the number you have in mind when you begin talking with potential employers. However, is this a realistic expectation?

Factors Affecting Compensation

Research indicates that salary expectations can be age related. Workers under forty-five, those in early mid-career, are more optimistic than older workers that they will find acceptable compensation packages. The reason is related to the amount of compensation in question. Younger workers usually have lower daily expenses and can afford to take a lower salary. Their tendency to take less makes their candidacy more appealing to potential employers. Workers over forty-five have more expenses and require more compensation to meet their needs.

For laid-off or fired workers seeking new employment, there is another factor at play, ego. Being let go is a devastating event, and laid-off workers subconsciously make every effort to salvage their self-respect. For example, when a mid-career worker is laid off from his manager-level job paying a base of $110,000, he expects to make that much or more going forward. His pride will not permit him to think it is okay to accept a job paying $90,000.

When my job candidates are evaluating an opportunity, I counsel them to be reasonable, not greedy, to remember that compensation is negotiable, and to accept the fact that nothing is guaranteed.

Responses to the Compensation Objection

Facing reality will save much time and angst and will hasten the job-hunting process. There is nothing that will jeopardize receiving a job offer more than believing, "I will not take less than $105,000, no matter what. That's what I made in my last job and that's what I'm entitled to get in my next job." That attitude reflects an entitlement mentality and does not match the reality of the workplace. Here's a true-life example of what can happen if you are delusional about compensation.

Janet from Philadelphia

One day in early January, Janet, a mid-career worker, came to my office. She was well dressed, articulate, and exuded an air of confidence. After pleasant introductory remarks, she told me that she had been working for a software company as an outbound sales representative for the past ten years and thought that she had earned a ticket to long-term employment. However, one afternoon the human resources director called her in for a chat. She told

Janet the company was being purchased by a competitor. It was an asset acquisition, and therefore her job was being eliminated. Janet was laid off that day and never saw it coming. Now she was on the street looking for another sales position. Her base salary was $130,000 and commissions averaged $80,000 per year. She asked me to help her find a sales position in the technology industry.

I asked Janet about her compensation expectations, and she told me she would not accept a penny less than her previous base. She expected a base of $130,000 and commissions that would average $80,000 per year, the same package as her last job. Knowing compensation numbers for such a position with companies in the area, I told Janet that her expectation was unrealistic because positions of that type were paying an average base of $100,000, and that commission plans varied greatly. She did not like what I told her and gave me a litany of reasons for her expectations. Four months later, Janet called to see what was happening. I told her that I did not have anything meeting her expectations and urged her to become more reasonable. In December of that same year, she came to my office again to inquire about job opportunities. It was almost a full year since she had been laid off, and she was still unemployed. Once again, I told her what the market was paying, and once again she would not lower her compensation demands. I could not persuade Janet to become more reasonable. After implying that I did not know my job, she left the office in a huff. She was still unemployed after almost a year of job hunting because she was delusional about her worth in the job market at that time.

Janet's story illustrates two points: that workers must be prepared to make compromises on compensation based on market conditions, and that workers must do their homework about compensation levels for their type of job. What Janet forgot is that the job market had changed since she joined her last employer ten years earlier.

Here are three compensation rubrics for all let-go workers to follow as they enter job-hunting mode.

Three Key Compensation Rubrics
1. Be open to compromise on compensation.
2. We do not live in an entitlement business culture. There is no guarantee that you will maintain or exceed rank, title, and compensation once you have reached a certain point in your career. It does not work that way in America.
3. Research compensation levels for your job type and rank remembering that compensation frequently varies with geography. A managerial position might average $150,000 per year in California, where the cost of living is very high, and $120,000 in Maine, where the cost of living is much lower.

SORRY! YOU DO NOT HAVE THE EDUCATION REQUIREMENTS FOR THIS JOB

It happens like this. You graduated from college with an AA, BA, or MA and proceeded to an entry-level job in your field of expertise. You work with this employer for five years and receive two promotions. Now you are working at the managerial level. Unexpectedly, one of your competitors comes to you with a job offer for a senior management-level position and an increase in compensation that puts you in the low-six-figure income bracket. "Nice," you think. "All of this without an MBA. Getting that college degree was a smart move on my part." So far, so good. You get married and have two children whose care takes all of your nonworking hours. Ten years later, you are still with the same company, have been promoted to a director-level position, and are making a base salary of $135,000, plus bonus and eligibility for the company profit-sharing program. Life is good. Then one ordinary day it happens. Your company is purchased by a competitor, and your position is eliminated.

Now you are out looking and have had only two interviews after three months of job searching. During an interview, the hiring manager tells you that your education background, especially in technology applications and project management is very weak compared to other candidates. He asks if you have taken any professional development courses over the past ten years. Your negative answer seals your fate. It is not that you were unaware of changes taking place in job requirements. You saw it coming, but you just did not have the time to update your skills.

The Education Solution

Much has changed since you received your last college degree, especially on the technology front. Younger and less experienced candidates have education credentials reflecting the change in workplace requirements. As soon as possible after being let go, begin taking certified online courses to plug the gap, particularly in the technology area. Make sure that your coursework provides written certification that you can present to potential employers. You can find certified online courses by conducting a Google search.

In my recruiting business, I have noted that many employers are requiring candidates for senior-level management positions to have project management professional training. It is commonly called PMP certification. PMP training is available online from a number of sources. One is the Project Management Institute (PMI), the world's largest source for training. It boasts having five hundred thousand members and 280 local chapters. Another online source for certification is Villanova University.

MOVING FORWARD

Before having your first phone or personal interview, plan how you will deal with the three most frequently encountered issues for mid-career job candidates: overqualification, compensation, and education. Do your homework on all three issues, because one or all could be part of your discussion with a hiring manager.

When you reach the job offer stage after overcoming objections to your candidacy, you could be confronted with issues spanning everything from base salary to non-compete requirements. We'll review all of this in the next chapter and provide guidelines about how to negotiate all parts of a job offer. This is an important part of the process, so stick around.

CHAPTER TAKEAWAYS

- Compensation levels for similar jobs will vary with geography.
- Overqualification is frequently a matter of perception on the part of the hiring manager.
- A certain compensation level is not guaranteed because of your experience or what you made in your last job.
- Technology moves fast in the workplace. Stay updated by taking online courses that carry certification.

PRINT AND DIGITAL RESOURCES

Bureau of Labor Statistics, www.bls.gov. Check this site for general compensation information.

Economic Research Institute, www.erieri.com. See ERI for compensation analysis by job and geography.

Profound Marketing Intelligence, www.profound.com.

Project Management Academy, www.projectmanagementacademy. net. The Academy offers online PMP certification.

The United States Census Bureau, www.census.gov. This site will keep you updated on job demographics and requirements.

Villanova University, www.villanovau.com/PMP. Villanova offers online PMP certification.

Chapter 15

NEGOTIATING A JOB OFFER

How many times have you heard on the street, "It costs too much"? This refrain usually pertains to the cost of goods and services. Sometimes it signals the beginning of the bargaining process. Take the street vendor in a big city like Chicago, Los Angeles, London, or New Delhi selling knock-off products like Ralph Lauren-labeled clothing or Coach-labeled purses or wallets. You don't pay the asking price. You negotiate.

The process is much the same when talking with a hiring manager or human resources director about a job offer. Many let-go candidates leave money on the table because they do not realize that the compensation part of a job offer is negotiable, except for government jobs that have a grade level and a corresponding compensation level. Moreover, let-go candidates are under pressure to bring home another paycheck and are inclined to accept whatever the first offer might be.

THE PROCESS FOR NEGOTIATING BASE SALARY AND BONUS

Think of the employer's office as a street vendor's stand where everything is negotiable: base salary, bonus, and possibly benefits. When you walk into the employer's office, whether it's a formal corporate office or a contractor's trailer at a commercial building site, imagine you are back on the street bargaining with a vendor of knock-off products. Here's what can happen.

Base Salary

The employer's HR person makes a base salary offer for a sales director's position. The human resources director says, "Tom, we are thrilled at the prospect of your joining us. I know you will be happy here. We'd like to make you an offer that consists of three parts: base salary, bonus, and benefits. Your starting base salary will be $120,000. Your bonus is 25 percent of base salary for exceeding your revenue goal by more than 10 percent. Your benefits include term life insurance equal to your base salary, three weeks of paid vacation, shared-cost medical and dental insurance for you and your family, long-term disability insurance, and a contributory IRA plan which becomes effective after ninety days. It's a generous offer, Tom. Here it is in writing. Could you let us know tomorrow when you can start?" You thank the human resources director and tell her you will come back tomorrow at ten after reviewing the offer.

Knowing the offer is low, you begin to compose a counteroffer. You have done your homework and know that comparable jobs in the area pay more than what was offered. In your last job, you had been making $140,000 base, plus a 10 percent bonus for meeting revenue goals, and benefits comparable to those in your new offer. Your research confirms that your evaluation is valid.

You really like the new job, the company, and its culture. This is a good place to be, and you decide to work out a compromise. You decide that you will try to negotiate a minimum base of $130,000, all factors considered, *including the fact that you have been laid off and the missing paycheck is beginning to take its toll on your pocketbook.* You are okay with the bonus and benefits. However, you would like to take an online course for PMP certification, the cost of which is $3,000.

You arrive at the office at ten and sit down with the HR director. Here is how you might present a counteroffer:

> I am flattered that you made me an offer to join the company. However, I have some thoughts about the base salary and one of the benefits. Based on my research for comparable jobs and considering my experience, I believe that a $150,000 base would be

equitable. I'm okay with the bonus. Also, I would like to continue my professional development by taking an online course for PMP certification, which would benefit the company. The cost is $3,000, and I would appreciate your including that in my compensation package.

The HR director can do one of three things: reject your counter-offer entirely, offer a compromise on your proposed base and the tuition, or concede entirely on your proposed base and tuition request. You must be prepared ahead of time for all subsequent counteroffers. Before you go into the office to negotiate, have a number in mind for the base you would accept, and a compromise on the tuition. If the HR director counters with a base of $125,000 and $2,000 on the tuition, you must be prepared to accept, counteroffer, or decline.

Does it really happen that way? You bet. Just a week before writing this, I presented a candidate to one of my clients for a director-level job that carried a base of $120,000, a $5,000 sign-on bonus, and $10,000 for relocation expenses. The candidate counteroffered and the company hiring manager came back with this final package: $125,000 base, a $10,000 sign-on bonus, and $15,000 for relocation expenses. He had offered the max that the company salary structure would allow. The result? The candidate said, "No, thank you" and accepted a job from another company offering a $150,000 base.

Bonus

Like base salary, a bonus can be negotiated. In fact, companies could be more flexible on bonus than on base salary. In some companies, certain workers receive a fixed bonus based on total company performance; in other companies, the bonus is based on individual or departmental performance. An exception is a bonus, or a commission as it is frequently called, for workers in sales.

Workers in sales receive a commission based on attaining revenue goals. For example, an outside full-time sales representative selling into the school market for John Wiley Publishing Company might receive 5 percent on all sales after reaching an established revenue quota of $2,000,000. If the sales rep delivers $2,800,000 ($800,000 over the revenue goal), the commission would be $40,000. If the sales representative's base salary was $60,000, the total income from base salary and commission would be $100,000, plus the value of the benefits, usually 30 percent of base, making the total package $118,000.

There are as many bonus and commission plans as there are companies. In small- to medium-sized companies, the bonus or commission plans are frequently negotiable. Large companies are usually not open to negotiation. The bottom line is this: always try to negotiate a higher bonus or commission. If the offer says the bonus or commission plan is 5 percent, ask for 8 percent. If the employer says no, ask for 6 percent. There is nothing to lose by asking. Your potential employer will probably appreciate that financial reward is an incentive for you, as it should be.

Everything monetary in a job offer is negotiable. In all of my experience in the staffing industry, I have never experienced a situation where the company did not have some flexibility on the money part of an offer.

BENEFITS PACKAGES

Traditional company benefits include medical and dental insurance, term life insurance, disability insurance, retirement plans such as an IRA (Individual Retirement Account), paid vacations, paid sick days, paid holidays, paid family leave, professional development education costs, tuition assistance for children, and unemployment compensation insurance.

Candidates often forget that benefits add to their compensation and to company expenses as well. Benefits are not "free." The entire benefits package must be monetized and added to the base salary in order to determine the *true* value of the offer. The current accepted price of all benefits to the employee averages 30 percent of base salary. For example, assume the base salary is $100,000. Add 30 percent for benefits, and your job is really worth $130,000. And if there is a stock option benefit and a company contributory IRA plan, you must include those items to arrive at your true compensation.

Which Benefits Are Negotiable?

A retirement program such as a company-sponsored IRA or Roth IRA will most likely become effective after you work with the company six to twelve months and cannot be negotiated. Paid holidays, paid sick leave, family leave, life insurance, disability insurance, and medical/dental insurance will not be negotiable. If they were, the company conceivably could have a different plan for each employee. However, vacation time is sometimes negotiable, or it can be used as a tradeoff for other benefits.

Your most important benefits are medical insurance and disability insurance, because one never knows when illness or an accident will strike. Medical and long-term disability insurance benefits are almost as important as base salary. Of course, these benefits have even greater importance if you are married and have children.

Healthcare

Prior to March 23, 2010, when the Affordable Care Act (Obamacare) became effective, a company would say, "Here is our medical and hospital plan. The plan is through Aetna and your benefits and costs are contained in this booklet." That is no longer the case. Multiple rules and regulations have been imposed on companies depending on their legal status, revenue, number of employees, and other factors. It's no longer one size fits all.

ACA has become a highly politicized piece of legislation, and as such there will be revisions going forward. A prudent thing to do now, however, would be to go online and research this important topic yourself because new information is becoming available every day through a number of different sources. Review the official website at www.healthcare.gov. Also, Google "Obamacare" and "Affordable Care Act," and you will find a number of sites providing valuable information.

Healthcare benefits are a matter for serious discussion with potential employers, so do not hesitate to ask for explanations about your options. The human resources director will be familiar with the provisions and will share them with you. Healthcare benefits, which include medical, dental, and eye-care insurance, will not be negotiable.

Profit Sharing
Some companies offer profit sharing in addition to, or in lieu of, a bonus plan. The higher the company profits in any given fiscal year, the higher the profit sharing for each employee. Some companies have a profit-sharing program based on total company revenue. If you do not see "profit sharing" in the job offer, always ask if you might be eligible to participate in the program. Most companies have a profit-sharing plan for their key executives, but might offer it as an incentive for mid-career workers who are applying for a management position. Some companies, like Starbucks or Texas Instruments, offer profit sharing for all employees regardless of rank.

Stock Options
Another benefit in publicly traded companies is the stock option plan. This benefit permits workers to purchase shares of company stock below market price. The number of shares an employee receives is directly proportionate to rank and length of time with the company. Presidents get more that vice presidents, who get more than directors, who get more than managers, and so on.

Companies offering attractive stock option plans usually have a workforce that is stable and long lasting. I have noted that workers in companies offering stock purchase plans retain workers for longer periods. For example, Apple provides a discounted stock purchase plan for its workers, which has created many millionaires. I know Apple employees who joined the company in 1980 and are still there, primarily because of the stock purchase plan.

Negotiating stock option plans is easier with a smaller company than it is with an established company like Google or Apple. The risk of continued long-term employment with a startup or small company is greater than that with an established company. For this reason, such small companies are more amenable to offering generous stock options to compensate workers for the added risk.

Tuition for Professional Development
Going forward, every worker will need to update their skills through professional development courses. They may be certification courses,

MA degrees, or even MBAs. Companies are usually open to including tuition reimbursement for such professional development because they benefit from your added knowledge and skills. Always ask for this benefit.

WHAT IS YOUR JOB REALLY WORTH?

Salary fluctuates with the economic cycle, workforce demand for a particular skill, and geography. For example, in a very robust economy where annual GDP growth is near 4 percent, compensation in a high-demand field, like information technology, will be higher than it would be when the country is in a steep recession.

One cannot reliably predict what a particular job will be worth in the future because of these variables, but there are many resources, both print and digital, for mid-career workers to use as a guide. On the print side, the most valuable resource is the *Occupational Outlook Handbook* which lists average salaries for jobs in a particular industry.

Periodically, conduct online searches for salary information because numbers change and new sources of information are always emerging. Review the following sites, remembering that the numbers you find are *estimates*, not firm and final data.

Sources for Determining Compensation

Salary.com, www.Salary.com.

PayScale, www.PayScale.com.

Bureau of Labor Statistics, www.bls.gov.

JobStar, www.JobStar.org.

CareerBuilder, www.careerbuilder.com/jobs-salary-comparison.

Occupational Outlook Handbook, www.bls.gov/oco.

SIX-FIGURE BASE SALARY JOBS

To put the compensation factor in context for mid-career workers who are negotiating job offers, I studied numbers released by the Bureau of Labor Statistics and confirmed by the *Wall Street Journal.* Here are the top twelve jobs paying six-figure base salaries.

Median Annual Wages for Occupations with Six-Figure Base Salaries

1. Physicians and Surgeons: $187,200
2. Chief Executive Officers: $175,110
3. Dentists: $158,310
4. Nurse Anesthetists: $157,140
5. Architectural and Engineering Managers: $132,800
6. Computer and Information Systems Managers: $131,600
7. Petroleum Engineers: $129,990
8. Pharmacists: $121,500
9. Natural Sciences Managers: $120,160
10. Podiatrists: $119,340
11. Marketing and Sales Managers: $119,280
12. Financial Managers: $117,000

Remember that these are median income numbers, which means that half are below and half are above the median income number stated.

Only twenty-seven occupations pay six-figure incomes. Management, healthcare, and engineering jobs account for twenty-two of the twenty-seven highest-paying occupations. Variables that still come into play are geography, total company revenue, education, and number of years of experience.

COMPANY COMPENSATION PARAMETERS

When negotiating base salary, bonus, and benefits, it is important to remember that the company must work within established parameters in order to keep peace in its workforce and maintain profitability. For example, assume that a company has a staff of twenty customer service representatives working from offices in Scottsdale, Arizona, all making a base salary in the $45,000 to $55,000 range depending upon length of service, experience, expertise, and education level. In that situation, it would be impossible to negotiate beyond $55,000. There would be a breakdown of trust if a customer service rep with two years of experience and making $40,000 learns that a new employee is making more. How will you learn the salary range for a particular position? Ask the director of human resources or the hiring authority with whom you are negotiating.

> **Basic Rules for Negotiating Base Salary, Bonus, and Benefits**
> Be reasonable. Be friendly. Be understanding.
> *Do not be greedy.*

EVALUATING THE SMALL PRINT CLAUSES IN A JOB OFFER

Frequently job offers contain a number of clauses that are overlooked because they are written in small print and in legal jargon. They just don't *seem* that important. However, it is critically important that you read and understand the small print provisions. They could affect your employment status, both short and long term. Here are the most frequent small print provisions found in a job offer.

Termination-at-Will Clause

Many job offers contain this provision. It means that the company, for no reason whatsoever, can terminate your employment. It can happen any day of the week when your boss or the human resources manager calls you into the office and says this is your last day working there. The real reason why you are being sacked could be that you did not perform up to expectations, and the most expeditious way to terminate your employment is to use business-speak, euphemisms like "downsizing," "rightsizing," or "reorganizing." Your job is not an entitlement, and in addition, you have no statutory right to your job.

Provisions of the termination-at-will clause will vary by state. Research the issue by Googling "Termination at will" and adding the state in which your company is located. If you want to be absolutely sure about how this provision will affect you, consult an attorney.

You can refuse to sign a job offer containing this clause, but your candidacy could be rejected because of it. I advise you to sign the offer agreeing to this clause and move on.

Non-Compete Clause

This clause means that you agree not to take a job with an employer that would be in competition with your company after you leave the company voluntarily or after being fired or laid off. Like the termination-at-will clause, state law governs the non-compete provision. Some states, like California, prohibit employers from using the non-compete clause in employment agreements.

Usually, this provision is time sensitive. Read the clause carefully. The non-compete time period could be limited to one year after separation from the company, or it could be forever. There is a geographical component to this clause as well. For example, the clause may prohibit you from working for a competitor located within a three-mile radius of your employer, or throughout the United States.

There is a disconcerting trend for employers to include stringent non-compete clauses and to increase strict enforcement by filing lawsuits against former employees who violate the agreement. Unfortunately, courts in a number of jurisdictions have ruled in favor of the company resulting in a severe fine against the employee. A recent article in the *New York Times* cited research about this controversial employment clause. The most disturbing news is that employers using the non-compete have expanded its scope to prohibit an employee from taking a job with another company working in the same or a related industry, or an employer whose operating procedures and infrastructure are similar. This means that if a worker is employed as an editorial director for a publishing company located in New York City, that worker is prohibited from taking a similar job with another publisher located anywhere in the United States for a stipulated number of years . . . or forever! Opponents of the non-compete argue that an employer has no right to control a worker's career and income, and we agree. The *Times* research cited a number of instances where an employee left the company for another job because it offered an increase in compensation and a move up the corporate hierarchy only to be served with a lawsuit to enforce a non-compete agreement. What such unscrupulous employers attempt to do is freeze workers into one job with one company during their entire working life.

If a job offer includes a non-compete clause that prohibits you from ever moving on *do not sign it*. If the employer will not negotiate this out of the offer, walk away from that company. However, if the job, the company, and compensation are in sync with your plans and you really do want the job, consult an attorney for advice.

There is an entire body of law governing the non-compete agreement. Google "Non-compete agreement" and add your state for current legislation.

Drug and Alcohol Testing Clause

There is a growing trend for companies to require a drug and alcohol screening as a condition of employment. Employers outsource these pre-employment tests. The potential employer always pays the bill for these screenings.

Refusing to submit to the pre-employment drug or alcohol screening will jeopardize your chances of employment. If you have nothing to hide, agree to the screening. However, what about Alaska, California, Colorado, Maine, Massachusetts, Nevada, Oregon, Washington, and the District of Columbia, where recreational use of marijuana is legal? Employers in these states still require the pre-employment screening and do not permit or condone use of federally defined illegal drugs and alcohol while on the job. If you live in one of these states, do not assume that employers permit the use of controlled substances. If you test positive for marijuana or any other controlled substance, you will not be hired.

Employers are very serious about this. For example, a sign written in bold letters on the entrance door of every Home Depot store in every state reads:

NOTICE
WE WILL TEST ALL APPLICANTS FOR ILLEGAL DRUG USE.
IF YOU USE DRUGS, DON'T BOTHER TO APPLY!

Federal law controls the use of recreational marijuana and other controlled substances, not state law, even though some states passed legislation permitting it. There is pending federal and state legislation on this. Don't test the waters. Agree to the drug provision or you will not be hired.

The Credit Check Clause

The credit check clause could be in the job offer for a number of reasons, the foremost of which is that employers do not want to deal with wage garnishment requirements. In addition, an employer may believe there is something lacking in a candidate's sense of responsibility if they have a history of unresolved debt or bankruptcy. If you have any long-term debt or substantial credit card debt, try to resolve these issues while in the search process. Do not object to the credit check clause. It could cost you a job. Just sign it and report to work.

The Starting Date Clause

A job offer will contain a start date. For example, assume you received the job offer on December 5 and it contains a start date of December 10. It sounds so official that you could be afraid of rejection if you do not agree to report on December 10 . . . even though you had a prepaid trip scheduled to see your ill mother halfway across the country. Do not fear the start date clause. All employers consider this a negotiable item.

The Relocation Clause

If a company offers you a job based in another location, the job offer may contain a relocation clause. The terms vary widely from company to company but usually they state how much the company will pay to relocate you, your dependents, your spouse or partner, and your household goods. There is much flexibility here and companies are willing to negotiate the terms of relocation. Relocation is a highly negotiable item and most companies will permit working remotely, even if the job is a presidency or vice presidency.

HOW TO REJECT A JOB OFFER

There is no rule that says you must accept a job offer, even if you have been laid off or fired. Some employers believe they can pick up a mid-career, laid-off worker "on the cheap" and will make a ridiculous offer. When that happens, reject the offer, because there are always other employers who will treat you fairly. How do you reject an offer? There are two ways to reject an offer after negotiations reach an impasse.

1. Tell the hiring manager that the job sucks and that you would be dumb to accept it.
2. Thank the hiring manager for considering your candidacy and wish him success finding an alternate candidate. Close the conversation by telling him that your rejection is nothing personal; it just does not provide what you need at this time.

The downside of using the first method is that you have severed the possibility of ever being considered for a future job opportunity at that company. In addition, the person on the other end of your message could move on to another company, and guess what? You will find no job opportunities at his new company.

The second method is the route to select when declining a job offer. It says that you have a sense of business etiquette, maturity, and good judgment. Your candidacy for another job opportunity will remain alive if you use the second method.

MOVING FORWARD

The cost for most products and services we purchase is negotiable. The same is true for base salary, bonus, and certain benefits found in job offers. American workers tend to believe that what is stated in a job offer is firm and final and never think to negotiate a better deal. Just the opposite is true.

Dr. Chester Karrass, author of four books on negotiating, tells how you can negotiate a job offer in his book *In Business As in Life, You Don't Get What You Deserve, You Get What You Negotiate*. Make time to read this book and two others by Karrass, titled

Give and Take and *The Negotiating Game.* These are classics, and Dr. Karrass will tell you what can be negotiated, how much can be negotiated, and how it is done.

Another step in the career rebuilding process is to determine where you would like to work. There are options like working in a large multinational corporation or a small neighborhood business. As an alternative, you could start your own business or purchase a franchise. All are viable options, and we'll explore them in part III, "Finding Your Spot in the Workplace." It's coming up next.

CHAPTER TAKEAWAYS
- The base salary part of the job offer is always negotiable.
- Drug and alcohol screenings are not negotiable.
- Make negotiations a friendly event.
- Be reasonable, not greedy.
- Decline a job offer politely.
- Do not sign a job agreement if it contains a highly restrictive non-compete clause. Walk away from the job or consult an attorney for advice.

PRINT AND DIGITAL RESOURCES
Carnegie, Dale and Associates. *How to Win Friends and Influence People.* Simon & Schuster, 2012.

Karrass, Chester. *In Business As in Life, You Don't Get What You Deserve, You Get What You Negotiate.* Stanford St. Press, 1996.

The official United States healthcare site is www.healthcare.gov.

Part III

FINDING YOUR SPOT IN THE WORKPLACE

I can get plenty of first violinists. But to find someone who can play the second fiddle with enthusiasm . . . that's a problem. And if we have no second fiddle, we have no harmony.

—Leonard Bernstein, the late conductor of the
New York Philharmonic Orchestra

Chapter 16

WORKING FOR A LARGE COMPANY OR A SMALL BUSINESS

M oving forward in the process of rebuilding your career, you have several choices: to work for a large company or a small business in the private sector, or to work in a government job. Working in a local, state, or federal government job has its own rules and challenges, so I have devoted chapter 18 to that topic. In addition, you have the option to start your own business or to purchase a franchise. Each initiative has its own challenges. Accordingly, we devoted all of chapter 17 to these topics.

Most laid-off workers lacking professional experience in specialized areas like medicine, law, or education, or who have no desire to start their own businesses, will in all probability exercise the default choice: working for a large company like Boeing, General Electric, or Facebook, or for a small business, one with fewer than five hundred employees. One is not better than the other. Large companies, called corporations if they have publicly traded stock, have much to offer including generous salaries and benefits like a contributory IRA and stock options, while small businesses require less work experience and formal education, and provide a more relaxed work environment. Pursuing one or the other is a matter of personal preference.

When mid-career workers are laid off or fired, they can continue working in the same industry or explore other industries. Workers usually exercise the second option when the industry where they spent the last fifteen years or more is undergoing a cyclical or structural change. For example, many editors, sales managers, marketing managers, and IT directors working for K-12 or higher-education publishing companies have been laid off as instructional materials are moving from print to digital delivery. Rather than continuing to pursue jobs in a changing industry, these mid-career workers have changed focus opting to seek employment in other industries. Take Judy, a regional sales manager in Chicago for a prominent K-12 publisher. When her job was eliminated, she came to me for counseling on the K-12 publishing industry and to explore sales manager positions with companies in other industries. After conducting her own due diligence and exploring industries in Chicago where she could transfer her sales skills, Judy decided to enter the real estate business, part of the broadly defined shelter industry. Now she is selling condos in the high-end market in downtown Chicago. She loves her new job in the shelter industry and is making a substantial six-figure income.

Contrary to street opinion, the majority of civilian workers are employed by small businesses, not large corporations like Amazon (647,000 employees) or Walmart (2.3 million employees). Regardless of their size, however, all companies fall into one of the major industries that keep our workforce employed. What are some of these industries? What are some of the companies in each industry? How large, or small, are they? Let's have a look at some of the major industries, broadly defined, because they provide plentiful job opportunities for mid-career workers. Here are some of the industries employing a large number of workers.

Major US Industries

- The Clothing Industry
- The Education Industry
- The Energy Industry
- The Financial Industry
- The Food Industry
- The Healthcare Industry
- The Insurance Industry
- The Petroleum Industry
- The Shelter Industry
- The Technology Industry
- The Transportation Industry

In addition, there are other fast-growing industries to explore, like the "Green Industry," which is concerned with making our local environment and planet Earth a more healthful and desirable place to live. The *Occupational Outlook Handbook* lists the following jobs associated with this industry:

- Biofuels Production Workers
- Biomass Energy Production Workers
- Energy Auditors
- Geothermal Energy Production Workers
- Hydroelectric Energy Production Workers
- Methane/Landfill Gas Production Workers
- Solar Energy Production Workers
- Weatherization Installers and Technicians
- Wind Energy Production Workers
- Environmental Restoration Planners
- Redevelopment Specialists and Site Managers
- Fuel Cell Technicians
- Industrial Ecologists
- Water Resource Specialists

Does "green" sound interesting? Get the *Handbook* and read more about these exciting and interesting opportunities.

TOP INDUSTRIES AND COMPANIES

The workplace is vast, and it takes a considerable amount of time to determine where to begin looking for a new job. First, learn the industry that best suits your interests and aptitude, and then look for companies within that industry. As you begin your exploration, consider the following criteria: industry importance to the US economy as a whole; the social value of its products and services; the projected industry rate of growth as measured by Standard & Poor's, a financial services research company; the job opportunities the particular industry provides now.

Here are some industries I consider a cut above the rest based on the criteria listed above, on personal experience working in the staffing business, on research, and on anecdotal information from a variety of sources:

- Education, especially the online sector and study abroad sector.
- Energy, particularly solar and nuclear.
- Healthcare/Pharmaceuticals, especially remote technology for diagnostic procedures, DNA testing and prognosis, and cancer treatments.
- Insurance, new policies to cover cybercrime.
- Security, protection against personal, corporate, and government hacking.
- Technology, especially artificial intelligence (AI) and robotics.
- Transportation, self-driving automobiles and trucks.

All are growth industries, and taken as a group, they employ tens of millions of workers. These seven industries offer endless job opportunities for all let-go workers who are moving forward in their careers and considering alternate industries for employment. Here is a brief review of each industry to set you moving in the right direction. Do remember that many of the job skills and leadership skills you acquired in your previous position are transferable to a job in a new industry.

The Education Industry

The broadly defined education industry consists of for-profit schools like DeVry Institute, Highlights for Children, McGraw-Hill Education, Pearson, Scholastic, and the University of Phoenix. There are nonprofits, too, like Educational Testing Service (ETS), Measured Progress, and The College Board.

These companies are scattered throughout the United States and offer jobs spanning the entire range of specialties like sales, marketing, finance, editorial, product development, information technology, and human resources. Workers in the education industry find much job satisfaction because the products are instructional materials and services for K-12, higher education, and adult education, which benefit individuals and the country as a whole. Some companies in this industry are:

- *Educational Testing Service (ETS),* www.ets.org
- *Highlights for Children,* www.highlights.com
- *McGraw-Hill Education,* www.mcgrawhill.com
- *Measured Progress,* www.measuredprogress.org
- *Pearson,* www.pearson.com
- *Scholastic,* www.scholastic.com

The Energy Industry

The energy industry is massive and includes petroleum companies, natural gas companies, LPG companies, nuclear energy companies, solar energy companies, and many others. This industry employs millions of workers in technical jobs that require very specific STEM (science, technology, engineering, and mathematics) skills and non-technical jobs requiring sales, marketing, and finance skills. This industry is noted for paying above-average wages and offering attractive benefits. Here are a several large companies to explore for job opportunities across the country.

- *ExxonMobil,* www.exxonmobile.com
- *Chevron,* www.chevron.com
- *Southwestern Energy,* www.southwesternenergy.com
- *ConocoPhillips,* www.conocophillips.com

The Petroleum Industry and Women

According to a recent Bureau of Labor Statistics (BLS) report, 46 percent of the new jobs in the petroleum business have gone to women. No, that is not a mistake. Check this out at www.bls.gov. Once again, the numbers tell it all. Regardless of your gender, religion, race, or ethnicity, go for any job in an industry that interests you. Work stereotypes are falling fast and the playing field is quite level. Don't fall for the hype. Always look at the numbers before drawing any conclusions.

The Healthcare and Pharmaceutical Industries

These two industries include pharmaceutical companies that produce prescription drugs and over-the-counter medications, medical device manufacturers, hospitals, and physical therapy treatment centers, just to name a few. These are robust industries that will see exponential growth as millions of baby boomers reach their senior years and require more frequent health services. Here are some of the more robust companies in this industry:

- *Cleveland Clinic,* www.my.clevelandclinic.org
- *Johnson & Johnson,* www.jnj.com
- *Medtronic,* www.medtronic.com
- *Pfizer,* www.pfizer.com

The list of companies could go on for several pages attesting to their vigor. In fact, *Fortune* magazine's list of the top one hundred companies to work for includes nineteen healthcare/pharmaceutical companies. In addition, *Fortune's* list of the ten best companies for women included the following seven healthcare companies. Go to their websites for more information.

Best Healthcare Companies for Women
- Atlantic Health System
- Baptist Health South Florida
- Children's Healthcare of Atlanta
- Meridian Health
- Novo Nordisk
- Scripps Health
- WellStar Health System

Work in the healthcare industry consists not only of medical professional jobs like physician, nurse, certified nurse midwife, and physical therapist, but also nonclinical jobs in sales, marketing, information technology, finance, and human resources. One does not need professional experience in clinical healthcare to work in this booming industry.

The Insurance Industry

Some consider this industry boring and concerned only with making money at the expense of policyholders. Who wants to do something as unexciting as working with policies for life insurance, auto insurance, homeowners insurance, short- and long-term disability insurance, flood insurance, and retirement instruments like annuities? Insurance is just an invention by greedy corporate executives to make money, right? Well, think again.

> **Thanks, Ben!**
> The insurance industry in the United States was founded by none other than Benjamin Franklin. He taught us that insurance is an instrument to minimize risk and deal with unforeseen occurrences, like a fire, that might consume your home and all of its contents. In so doing, Ben gave birth to an industry where it is almost impossible to fail, one that employs some of the most brilliant mathematical minds on earth. These mathematical geniuses are the actuaries. They deal with massive amounts of data to determine risk levels and then price insurance policies accordingly.

Insurance products have become a necessity to live as a responsible, self-sufficient human being. Insurance policies provide monetary benefits to policyholders who suffer misfortunes, whether it is an illness that costs thousands of dollars to treat or an accident that causes temporary or permanent disability resulting in loss of wages, which in turn can cause inestimable hardship. Insurance provides numerous and varied job opportunities in sales, marketing, technology, finance, human resources, underwriting, and highly technical jobs as well. Here are some of the best in the industry based on general reputation for integrity, financial strength, longevity, and community outreach:

- *MassMutual,* www.massmutual.com
- *Northwestern Mutual,* www.northwesternmutual.com
- *State Farm,* www.statefarm.com

- *USAA,* www.usaa.com
- *Unum,* www.unum.com

The Security Industry

The security industry has been growing exponentially because of cybercrime against government agencies and private companies. Hacking of both American government and corporate websites by criminals from foreign countries seems to make the news every day. Companies in the security industry undertake a wide variety of initiatives, however: preventing cheating on exams; securing private property; protecting financial information; protecting confidential data, both private and governmental; and reducing the threat of terror attacks. There are many companies in the security industry, and each limits its activities to one or two specialties. Here are two examples:

- *Caveon,* www.caveon.com. This company focuses on preventing cheating on tests and test scores in K-12 schools and colleges.
- *Raytheon,* www.raytheon.com. This American icon located in the Boston area is a leader in cybersecurity for both industry and government.

The Technology Industry

Technology moves at the speed of light, and there are always companies coming and going in the technology business. Working for a technology startup can be exciting but carries substantial risk. A safer bet is to look at established technology-driven companies. Here are some of the best:

- *Salesforce.com,* www.salesforce.com
- *Amazon,* www.amazon.com
- *Adobe,* www.adobe.com
- *Nvidia,* www.nvidia.com
- *Facebook,* www.facebook.com

The Transportation Industry

This industry includes companies that produce automobiles, airplanes, boats, trains, railroads, trucks, and bicycles, and companies that offer support items like tires, batteries, rails, seats, and windows. Many interesting companies fit into this category and many are household words. One thing is certain in this world in addition to death and taxes: there will always be a need to move people and goods from one place to another. Here is a sampling of prominent and respected transportation companies:

- *Boeing,* www.boeing.com
- *Hertz,* www.hertz.com
- *Lockheed Martin,* www.lockheedmartin.com
- *Southwest Airlines,* www.southwest.com
- *Tesla,* www.tesla.com
- *Toyota,* www.toyota.com
- *Union Pacific Railroad,* www.unionpacific.com

Do not overlook this booming industry. It offers jobs throughout the country, good jobs with security, attractive wages, and excellent benefits.

TOP-RANKED LARGE COMPANIES: ENTERTAINMENT, FINANCE, FOOD, RENTAL, TECHNOLOGY

The usual route that many let-go workers follow is to look on the job boards and scour social media for leads to job opportunities with *any* company that may be hiring.

There is a better way to find good potential employers. Search for companies that have been in business for many years and that have been profitable. Target companies whose products and services are in constant demand throughout the business cycle, and which have a good reputation with their workers for fair play. Why spend your time throwing darts at the entire board of American companies?

To start you headed in the right direction, here is a list of prominent companies in various industries. It is not by any means a complete list, but it will give you an idea of important characteristics and criteria for assessing employers. Note that this list includes companies that produce tangible products and companies that provide services.

- **The Blackstone Group,** www.blackstone.com. This is one of the world's leading investment and financial advisory firms. It is headquartered in New York City, with eight regional offices spread throughout the country and offices abroad as well. Blackstone services include management of corporate private equity funds, real estate opportunity funds, hedge funds, mezzanine funds, senior debt vehicles, proprietary hedge funds, and closed-end mutual funds. The company has a solid reputation for treating its employees and customers fairly. In addition, it contributes millions of dollars to community charitable organizations.
- **Coca-Cola,** www.coke.com. This one-hundred-year-old company has provided jobs for millions of people not only in the United States, but also throughout the world. Coke treats its workers well and is in reorganization mode. Many of Coke's workers are nearing retirement age, and mid-career workers are taking over. They have new ideas, use technology effectively, and are positioning Coke to reach new levels of performance and revenue.
- **Costco,** www.costco.com. Costco employs 174,000 workers, most working behind the scenes in real estate, finance, marketing, technology, supply chain management, purchasing, construction, online retail sales, and human resources. Working at Costco is not only about stocking shelves and working the cash register. Management jobs are plentiful, from local store managers to IT directors at the corporate and regional levels. But there is more to the Costco story. Among big box retailers, Costco ranks number one in wages paid to store employees, $21 per hour. Costco sells more wine than any other company in the world, and that's not all. Costco sells more than 140 million rotisserie chickens and 150 million hot dogs each year. Hungry for a good job, a

hot dog, a rotisserie chicken, and a nice bottle of wine from the Loire Valley in France? Work at Costco. As Costco grows and opens more stores it will need more mid-career workers at the store and corporate levels to manage an expanding workforce.

- *Disney,* www.disney.com. This iconic company is part of the entertainment industry and provides job opportunities throughout the world. Check out the website to review a variety of openings spanning everything from sales to human resources. Disney has a reputation for being an employee-friendly company and for supporting community programs.

- *Dow Chemical,* www.dow.com. Dow products are used in almost every facet of our lives. The company has grown exponentially worldwide and has won many "best employer" awards in countries around the world. Many consider Dow one of America's best employers because of its reputation for creating a diverse workforce where everyone is welcome. Dow employs over 55,000 workers and has sales revenues of approximately $60 billion. Dow is merging with DuPont.

- *General Electric,* www.generalelectric.com. GE, founded in 1892, has its fingers in many manufacturing pots and is undergoing a massive reorganization with a new CEO. GE is a multinational conglomerate, which means that it manufactures and produces a multitude of products that are sold in many countries. Many GE products, such as power plants and engines, are used by the US military. The company has an excellent record for philanthropy and community outreach and for promoting from within. The company is quickly carving out a niche in technology while maintaining its manufacturing profile.

- *General Mills,* www.generalmills.com. "Wheaties. Breakfast of Champions." General Mills has been serving up this breakfast cereal in its iconic orange box, which highlights professional and college athletes, for the past eighty years. The company is doing a lot right like producing foods that customers enjoy and find nutritious. General Mills employs forty-one thousand workers and generates $18 billion in annual sales. It has created a diverse workforce, pays its employees well, is active in community outreach and usually promotes management level workers from within.

- *Home Depot,* www.homedepot.com. Where else can you find houseplants, light bulbs, home appliances like dishwashers, and sheets of plywood for home construction under the same roof? This is a very profitable company with locations across the US and abroad. The company employs 365,000 workers and has annual revenues exceeding $100 billion. As the real estate market grows so does Home Depot. Whenever someone buys a house, they always need fix-up products and the most convenient place to find those products at fair prices is this company. Its stock price has grown substantially, reflecting shareholder confidence that this company is headed in the right direction.

- *IHG,* www.IHG.com. The InterContinental Hotels Group includes famous names like Holiday Inn, Holiday Inn Express, InterContinental Hotels, Crown Plaza, and others. On their career page, you will find hundreds of jobs listed by job title and location, both domestic and international. IHG has hotels in eighteen countries and counting, and has increased its number of hotels in the United States. Each new facility creates more jobs and greater rewards for its shareholders. It is in acquisition mode which means they are growing and hiring new management-level employees.

- *Johnson Controls,* www.johnsoncontrols.com. Johnson Controls is the world's leading provider of control mechanisms for the building and automotive industries. Annual revenues exceed $42 billion. Your automobile could not run without their products. Johnson is a technical organization and has a constant need for employees having a STEM background. As building and transportation initiatives, like driverless cars, increase, so will jobs for mid-career workers.

- *Lowe's,* www.lowes.com. A WWII veteran, Carl Buchan, founded this major home supply company, which has a reputation for treating its employees like family. In addition, Lowe's is customer focused and community conscious. As with all large retailers, most of the jobs at Lowes are located off the floor.
- *McDonald's,* www.mcdonalds.com. This company is expanding its fast food menu constantly and is located in almost every country on the planet. It has been in business for over sixty years and employs approximately two million workers in one hundred countries. Annual revenues are approximately $30 billion. McDonald's is noted for supporting community outreach activities, especially those related to children.
- *Qualcomm,* www.qualcomm.com. This company is a global semiconductor designer and a manufacturer and marketer of digital wireless telecommunications products. It is one of the best in the business and has been around since 1985, a long time in the technology business. Qualcomm is based in San Diego and employs thirty thousand workers. The demand for all types of semiconductors is growing exponentially and Qualcomm is considered by industry analysts to be well positioned to meet that need. In addition, the company has a reputation for community service in California and provides special employment opportunities for military veterans.
- *Salesforce.com,* www.CRM.com. This is the preeminent cloud-computing company headed by a highly respected CEO, Mark Benioff. Recently the company created a nonprofit division targeting the higher-education market. The stock price has been increasing steadily because company revenues have been increasing and investors consider Salesforce.com to be the best of breed. The company has an excellent track record of service to the community and contributes to worthy causes. Recently it has formed strategic relationships with Amazon and IBM. More jobs will follow.
- *Starbucks,* www.starbucks.com. A few years ago, people asked, "What can a coffee house do for America? What's all the fuss about another coffee joint?" Well, for starters,

a good cup of joe in the morning is the traditional way that most Americans begin their day. It is part of our culture. A cup of morning coffee is just as much a part of our culture as is the demitasse cup of super strong espresso that the Italians drink before going to work. However, there is more to this story than drinking coffee.

Starbucks has provided both part-time and full-time jobs for millions of Americans from coast to coast, and it treats its workers fairly. Many workers who start as baristas (don't you love the job title?) move up to executive level management positions. In addition, the former CEO, Howard Schultz, has made a concerted effort to bring jobs back to America by using only American manufacturers to provide essential items such as paper coffee cups, which are manufactured in Ohio. In 2015, Starbucks initiated an online college scholarship program for all employees.

Starbucks has a bright future and we recommend that you check out the website for job opportunities. You will see jobs in supply chain operations, finance, global development, information technology, retail sales, coffee roasting operations, and many others.

- *Texas Instruments,* www.ti.com. TI is eighty years old. It is not a Johnny-come-lately to the technology world, and it produces more than calculators. TI produces technology products like RFID barcodes, and sophisticated semiconductors, those little beasts that make your digital toys run. TI has a presence in thirty-five countries, and employs thirty-five thousand workers. Annual revenues top $14 billion. The company is based in Dallas, Texas, and has offices scattered throughout the United States and abroad.

  TI has a reputation for treating its workers like family despite its size, which explains why people work there for many years. TI has one of the best mentoring programs in the business, and one of its most attractive benefits is a profit-sharing program that has made many workers very wealthy.

- *Tiffany & Co.,* www.tiffany.com. This American icon of upscale jewelry and fine home furnishings has been in business since 1837. Do you want to work in a pleasant environment surrounded by beautiful objects of art for the home and personal adornment? Do you get high looking into a flawless two-carat diamond? If you answer "yes" or even "maybe," the next step is to review the career pages on the Tiffany website.

- *United Rentals,* www.unitedrentals.com. This is one of the largest tool and equipment rental companies in the world and offers many interesting opportunities for mid-career workers. As our economy continues to grow, so does the demand for construction equipment. United Rentals offers generous employee benefits and will continue to grow as our country embarks on a new round of infrastructure rebuilding.

- *Verizon,* www.verizon.net. The country's largest wireless carrier offers employment opportunities in all states and is at the forefront of all forms of digital communication. The array of jobs with this communication giant is impressive. It is very employee friendly and enjoys a reputation for promoting from within.

- *Whole Foods,* www.wholefoods.com. This company deserves an A+ for leading America toward better eating habits by selling organic foods that are free from chemicals and pollutants, which are harmful to our health. In addition, the CEO is committed to working with the community to provide assistance to those who need a basic item for survival—food. Based in Austin, Texas, Whole Foods is one of the most socially responsible companies in the world. The company employs approximately sixty thousand workers and annual revenue tops $12 billion. *Fortune* magazine ranks Whole Foods in the top one hundred best companies for workers. Whole Foods has an excellent benefits program for its employees and offers a career path for workers seeking long-term employment. Whole Foods has been purchased by Amazon.

These are just a few of the large companies that hire millions of workers each year. When you explore any company, focus first on the company's financial strength and its projected growth rate by industry analysts. If you like what you see, explore the career pages and apply for a position that matches your profile. Remember to send your resume and career profile to the human resources director or department hiring manager by name. Never send career information to "Employment Manager" or "Position #257." *The job-hunting process includes building a relationship with a named person who is in a position of authority to hire job candidates such as you.*

SMALL BUSINESSES ARE BIG EMPLOYERS

The Bureau of Labor Statistics defines small businesses as those companies employing fewer than five hundred workers. There are 28 million small businesses in America, and they employ over 50 percent of all workers. Approximately 543,000 small businesses are started each year. A small business can be anything from a corner deli employing three or four workers to a niche technology firm with several hundred workers.

Working for a small business, as opposed to a large company like one of those listed above, offers both considerable advantages and considerable challenges. Many small businesses have greater sensitivity to disruptions in the economic climate. They are subject to going out of business at the first hiccup in the economy because they depend on month-to-month revenue to stay alive. (Large companies usually have cash reserves to carry them through lean times, or they have readily available sources to borrow money.)

Generally, working for a small business carries more risk for workers than working for a large corporation. Small business owners usually do not have the resources to provide salaries and benefits offered by large firms, even for their managerial-level employees. Some small businesses do not offer retirement plans, such as a 401K or IRA, and their benefits packages may offer only legally required medical and hospital insurance. Compensation is usually less in a small business than it is in a large corporation.

On the plus side of the equation, small businesses can be more flexible in providing personal time off and more relaxed work rules. Usually the culture is friendlier and employers are more flexible on job requirements. Previous work experience and formal education requirements are not as rigid as they are in a large company.

Owners of small businesses usually carry out the hiring process personally while large companies hire recruiters to conduct candidate searches or post their openings on numerous job boards. The hiring process in a small business is abbreviated. Frequently, a job candidate receives an offer after the first personal interview. The hiring process with a large company can be onerous and take sixty to ninety days, or more, beginning to end. The reason is that more company personnel are involved in the decision-making process, and they have more candidates in the vetting process for a particular position. In a small business, the hiring manager could be your potential boss or the president of the company.

SOURCES FOR EVALUATING COMPANIES

Mid-career workers in transition should devote time and attention to a complete and impartial evaluation of any potential employer. In addition to hearsay, trusted networking sources, and social media chatter, there are sources that provide objective reports on any company you are considering for employment. Here are two reliable Internet resources for locating information about companies that interest you. All of them provide financial information, company product information, and industry standing.

1. *Investopedia,* www.investopedia.com
2. *Hoover's,* www.hoovers.com

NOTE ON LEADERS AND FOLLOWERS

Regardless of the employer and its size, all workers fall into two categories, leaders and followers. Where you want to go is a matter of choice. One is not better than the other.

The media is filled with hype about becoming a leader and how one should acquire leadership skills. Little is ever said about followers, but one cannot exist without the other.

Leaders seem to get our attention, but they would not be successful if they did not have skilled followers. It is nothing less than a symbiotic relationship. For example, a vice president for sales will be successful only if the followers, the territory sales representatives, bring in the orders.

However, all leaders must be good followers as well. For example, a marketing director is a leader who not only has direct reports to manage, but also is a follower of the boss, the vice president for marketing or the president. Regardless of your rank as leader, you will always be a concurrent follower, unless you are the sole owner of the company.

Skills Required for Good Leaders and Followers

Mid-career workers who aspire to higher levels of management must acquire certain skills and personal qualities to inspire, mentor, and motivate their followers to attain goals. Some of these required skills are clear and concise written and verbal communication, delegating authority, planning, prioritizing, vision, honesty, commitment, adaptability, and relationship building.

A dictionary definition of a follower reads, "One who accepts the teachings of another." Mid-career workers who would rather take the path of follower must possess job skills and social skills, too. Some of these are: loyalty, knowledge of the company products and services, passion for completing the mission, adherence to the rules and regulations laid down by the leader (i.e., the boss), intelligence to learn the details of the mission, patience, and honesty.

MOVING FORWARD

The usual path mid-career workers take is to find employment with another company in the same industry. However, they have the option of changing industries, or doing something else like saying goodbye to a large company or small business employer and starting one's own business, an attractive option for many laid-off workers. I will lead you through the process in the next chapter.

CHAPTER TAKEAWAYS

- All companies and small businesses are part of a larger entity called an industry.
- The hiring process for a large company is more detailed and lengthier than it is for a small business.
- A record of community outreach is one important factor in evaluating a company.
- Companies with a long record of profitable operations are usually good employers.
- Being a good follower is just as important as being a good leader.

PRINT AND DIGITAL RESOURCES

Adair, Troy, PhD. *Corporate Finances Demystified*. McGraw-Hill, 2011.

Cramer, Jim. *Jim Cramer's Real Money*. Simon & Schuster, 2009.

"Customized Industry Reports." Profound. www.marketresearch. com. This site provides company research reports and industry analyses.

Dun & Bradstreet. www.dnb.com.

Fortune magazine. *Fortune* is published monthly, print or digital, at a reasonable cost to subscribers.

Hoover's. www.hoovers.com.

SmartBrief on Leadership. www.smartbrief.com/industry/business/ leadership. This site provides articles on leadership and business generally authored by its own writers and outside sources as well.

US Department of Labor. *The Occupational Outlook Handbook*. JIST Publishing, 2016-2017.

Chapter 17

STARTING YOUR OWN BUSINESS OR BUYING A FRANCHISE

For most workers seeking a new beginning in mid-career, the thought of starting a business is intriguing, but how do you toss the first pitch in this ball game? Street talk tells only the stories of entrepreneurs who dropped out of college, locked themselves in a garage for a couple of years, and then emerged with a business called Apple Computer or Microsoft or Virgin Air. Continue listening to the street, and you hear that it can happen only if you are rich, famous, or have significant family connections.

Reality is much different. Any mid-career worker with intelligence, energy, and passion can start their own business by following a few simple rules and listening to successful entrepreneurs like Elon Musk, founder and CEO of SpaceX and cofounder of Tesla Motors; Richard Branson, founder of Virgin Air; Chris Weiss, founder and owner of RaffertyWeiss Media; and Ruth Fertel, founder of Ruth's Chris Steak House chain.

As you begin exploring this initiative, make your first stop the US Small Business Administration (SBA), www.SBA.gov. The SBA provides information in nontechnical language about how to start and operate your business and make money in the process.

WHO STARTS A NEW BUSINESS?

Join the thousands who have started their own businesses instead of working for someone else. The fact that you have a wide array of skills learned in your previous jobs, a college degree, or both, does not mean that you are destined to work for a big corporation or a small business. Working for a company, particularly a large one, where the ground rules can be oppressive, may not be your idea of a good time. The alternative is to start your own business.

What must you do before hanging out a sign with your name on it? Isn't it true that most business owners have money in the family and are mostly upper class? To clear up those misconceptions, here is the profile of people who start their own businesses according to an article that appeared in the *Wall Street Journal*.

Who Starts a New Business?

Less than 1 percent of people who start a business comes from extremely rich or extremely poor backgrounds. 71.5 percent come from a middle-class background. 70 percent used their own savings as the source to fund their own businesses.

So much for the stereotypes of business owners. I like numbers. They usually set the record straight.

PORTRAITS OF SUCCESSFUL BUSINESS OWNERS

Who are some of these successful entrepreneurs? Are there any good examples of workers who decided to make it on their own instead of casting their lot with a company? The answer is a resounding "yes." Here is an inspirational story written by a mid-career worker who left corporate work and did it his own way.

Captain Kiel King of New York (US Army Ret.)

First, I am medically retired as an Army Captain. Upon returning to the United States from Germany, I spoke with the Lucas Group, an executive recruiting firm, which provided job leads, including one at Coca-Cola. My bachelor's degree is in chemistry & life sciences from West Point, but it did not come into play while taking my interview with the Coca-Cola Bottling Company. I was hired after the first interview. I started with Coca-Cola as a production manager a month after leaving the military. But, after one year, I found that I was working in a field that I did not enjoy. I believe I was hired due to my leadership experience in the Army and my education at West Point. After a bit of soul searching, I decided it was important to continue my education in an area that I truly loved, and went back to school to complete a graduate degree in physical rehabilitation sciences. I have since started my own company called Kings of Fitness, where the mission is to educate, motivate, and inspire individuals to live a healthy and physically active lifestyle. While I was in the Army, helping people was extremely important to me, and now that I am medically retired, helping people is still the most important thing that gives me true job satisfaction. I did not have that with Coca-Cola.

Here is what we can learn from Captain King:

- Education must continue at all stages in one's career.
- There are sources of help available for entrepreneurs.
- Start a business that grabs your interest and provides meaning for your life.
- Define the mission.
- Plan your work. Work your plan.

HOW TO GET STARTED

The rules of business entrepreneurship apply equally to everyone. There are not two sets of rules. Consider what Richard Branson said in his first blog entry for LinkedIn, posted in 2012: "As LinkedIn is a business that started in a living room, much like Virgin which began in a basement, I thought my first blog on the site should be about how to simply start a successful business." Here are Branson's five top tips:

1. Listen more than you talk.
2. Keep it simple.
3. Take pride in your work.

4. Have fun, success will follow.
5. Rip it up and start again.

These are the first steps that Richard Branson took when founding one of the most successful businesses on the planet. Branson always has good ideas for entrepreneurs and has authored twelve books about starting businesses and operating them profitably. I've listed two of them in the resources at the end of this chapter.

Go to LinkedIn periodically and read Branson's blogs. You will receive advice from one of the world's most successful business owners at a terrific price—*free*. We can learn much from him. He's been there, done that without a college degree, without family money, while working from a basement office. He planned his work and worked his plan. Success followed.

MORE FAMOUS ENTREPRENEURS

If you explore how other entrepreneurs founded their businesses, their stories will be similar to Branson's. For example, in 2005 Arianna Huffington founded the *Huffington Post*, which has become an American media icon. She sold the *Post* to AOL for $315 million but still plays an active role as editor. Her net worth is estimated to be $50 million.

Steve Jobs and Steve Wozniak both dropped out of college after their first year and founded Apple Computer . . . working out of a garage. Then we have Larry Ellison, founder and CEO of Oracle, who bypassed college altogether and founded one of the world's largest software companies. His net worth is close to $50 billion. What does he do with his money? Several years ago, he purchased the entire island of Lanai in the Hawaiian Islands. Yes, the *entire island*, not just a couple of acres. He still has plenty of money left over, much of which he donates to charitable causes.

And let's not forget Mark Zuckerberg, founder and CEO of Facebook, another person with big dreams and little appetite for continuing his education at Harvard. He dropped out of college and founded Facebook. Mark is in mid-career and his start-up, Facebook, is a publicly held company with more than two billion users. Mark's net worth is over $50 *billion*. He and his wife contribute hundreds of millions of dollars to charitable causes.

I WANT TO DO IT MY WAY

These successful businesses all began as someone's dream, which was refined into a viable business while working from a garage or basement. (I'm not sure why garages and basements are so attractive for entrepreneurs. That's just the way it is.) Captain Kiel King, Bill Gates, Steve Jobs, Steve Wozniak, Larry Ellison, and Mark Zuckerberg could do it, and so can you. The business you start does not have to be another Microsoft in order to be successful. There are thousands of small businesses founded, owned, and operated successfully by someone who had the courage to say, "I want to do it my way." Here is another story of such an individual.

Colonel Harland Sanders

Harland Sanders was born in 1890 and spent the first forty years of his life working in a variety of jobs. As a child, he learned to cook family-style meals from his mother while working on a farm. In 1902, he enlisted in the Army and was honorably discharged after serving his country. He had no clear career path and bounced from job to job working primarily for railroads. At nights, he worked on a law degree by mail correspondence from La Salle Extension University, a forerunner of today's online universities. After practicing law for a brief time, he accepted an offer from the Shell Oil Company to operate a gas station in Corbin, Kentucky. A true multitasker, Harland began cooking and selling meals from his own house adjacent to the gas station. One of his specialties was chicken, not fried or baked, but cooked in a new device called a pressure cooker. Word spread that Sanders chicken was the best you could buy, and he gave up the gas station business and opened restaurants that featured his specialty, chicken. At about the same time, the governor of Kentucky commissioned Harland as a Kentucky Colonel, an honorary title. In 1940, Harland created and promoted his "secret recipe" for his now-famous chicken, attracting rave notices from food critics who spread the word nationwide. In 1952, he franchised his first restaurant and named it Kentucky Fried Chicken. The rest of this story is history.

Harland Sanders's story proves that successful entrepreneurs do not have to be technology gurus like Gates or Zuckerberg. Any smart mid-career worker using their intelligence, energy, and passion can do the same. If the thought of founding a company that has your name on sounds exciting, go for it! There are many books and websites offering ideas about how to get started and there are many support groups ready to help entrepreneurs accomplish their goals.

Starting Your Own Business As a Sole Proprietor

Can you really start your own business, as did Sanders, Zuckerberg, and Gates? How long does it take before you can make serious money to become self-sufficient? What kinds of businesses are there?

Many entrepreneurs have founded successful small businesses. Where are they? Take a walk down Main Street, USA, and talk with the owner of a storefront business, and you will get the answer. For now, look at several small businesses that were started by people who had a dream and ambition.

Gary from Philadelphia

I was looking for someone to wash the windows at our home in suburban Philadelphia. Fortunately, we found Gary through a referral from a neighbor. The job took Gary about six hours and we paid him $400, which translates into $66 per hour. We have employed Gary for the past seven years. He begins work at the appointed hour, supplies all window-cleaning products, and maintains the high quality of work. Recently, Gary added another service to his business—residential exterior power washing—which is a perfect complement to the window washing business.

I can hear the snickering now. Window washing with a college degree? You have to be kidding! Well, what if I told you that Gary's business generates a revenue stream comparable to that of a corporate manager and that he works only ten months of the year? (Gary works only ten months because inclement weather in January and February prevents him from working outside.) Now what do you think about the residential window washing business? Compare that to a corporate job. An average mid-career corporate job will bring in about $135,000 per year. You will get three weeks' vacation, report to work each day at a specific time, and will work in a corporate people kennel, also called a cubicle. You will be on call 24/7 and have little time to call your own. Gary, on the other hand, makes an annual six-figure income, works on his own terms, and reports to a boss named . . . Gary.

So what is Gary's background? What kind of education do you need to start your own business? Here's the rest of the story. Gary graduated from Temple University in Philadelphia with a bachelor's degree in business administration and began working in the corporate world. One of his employers was General Electric, where he held a managerial position. He was not happy and decided to make it on his own. He researched several business possibilities and found there was no competition in the residential window washing business. He started his own window washing business with a modest investment and a few years later had several people working for him.

Gary's story is about how to make a living on your own terms. Owning and operating your own business is one of the most satisfying things you can do. Your business will provide a good income, the option to work on your own terms, and time to give back to the community by participating in your choice of outreach programs. The term "work" does not always mean putting in time with a Fortune 500 company. Gary's work is not window washing. *His work is running a service business that he calls his own.*

Consulting Businesses

Frequently, laid-off workers start their own businesses as consultants working in a variety of roles in a particular industry. They undertake specifically defined assignments for a certain period of time. After completing an assignment, they move on to another. It is a quick and inexpensive way to put the past behind and continue generating income. If your past career focused on marketing in the publishing business, make that the focus of your consulting business and seek assignments from your contacts in the industry. Some workers make consulting a full-time occupation instead of returning to a managerial-level corporate job.

Another reason why some let-go mid-career workers hang out their own shingle as consultants is to remain business-active while seeking new full-time opportunities. In addition to providing much-needed income, consulting provides opportunities to build new business relationships. Newly minted consultants usually do this by attending conferences at major convention centers where they frequently find new business clients.

Starting a consulting business is not complicated, but it takes courage. Here is a list of guidelines to begin your own consulting business:

- Decide what kinds of assignments you can complete successfully. For example, if you have experience managing a sales team, seek assignments from companies in your industry who might need part-time sales help to introduce a new product to a specific group of potential customers.
- Name your company. It need not be fancy. "James Henry, Marketing Consultant" works well.
- Set up an email address, a Twitter account, and a Facebook account reflecting your new consulting business.
- Construct a website. You can do this on your own or have an online source construct it for you. However, if you are just biding your time while seeking another full-time corporate job, you can skip this step in the process.
- Purchase business cards. It sounds elementary but you will need something for identification when you are seeking customers and building your network at conferences.
- Contact your former employer(s) to solicit business as an independent consultant. Frequently workers who have been laid off because of budget cuts find part-time assignments from their former employer.
- Attend conferences in your industry at local convention centers and visit each exhibit booth to solicit business.

Starting a Business with a Partner

Another way to start your own business is with a partner who has interests and values similar to yours. Selecting the *right* partner is an important first step and requires a complete examination of that person's skills, energy, intelligence, passion for self-employment, ethics, values, and interest in the ideas you have for starting a business. Researching your potential partner is critical. If you select just a good friend instead of a *good business friend* who is compatible with you in every way, your business could turn into a nightmare. Many entrepreneurs have failed because they selected the wrong partner.

Here is a good example of a successful partnership, in the words of a successful businessman, Chris.

Chris from Silver Spring, Maryland

I worked as a video producer at a large telecommunications corporation for approximately five years. I stayed there longer than I wanted to as I waited first for stock options to increase in value. When that didn't happen, I waited to see if I could obtain a buyout package. That didn't happen either, but I decided to leave because the company was in trouble. It was just a matter of time before I could be let go.

I talked to a freelance producer, Patrick Rafferty, whom I had met when he worked at the same company but on a contract basis. We seemed like a good fit. We got along well personally and we both had a similar amount of experience in the profession. What sold us on each other was that while we had some overlap in terms of our strengths, in other areas my strengths complemented his weaknesses, and vice versa. To test our compatibility as business partners, we decided to start working together on projects as independent entities.

Our first year as a company was lean, even though we had a number of contacts around town. We each took in about $30,000 gross that first year, which would not have been sustainable for either of us for much longer. However, business picked up in the second year, and our revenues have increased substantially every year after that. In January 2017, we began our sixteenth year working together as a partnership in the video production business. Our company is RaffertyWeiss Media.

The video production business is not for the faint of heart. It requires exceptional written and verbal communication skills, bottom-line business skills, creativity, imagination, and technical expertise. While Chris possessed all of those qualities, the time requirements for operating a successful media business as a sole proprietor are significant. When Chris found a partner with similar values and skills, he founded RaffertyWeiss Media.

Starting Your Own Business with a Franchise

Another way to start your own business is to purchase a franchise. Franchises focus primarily on products and services related to the big three survival industries: food, shelter, and clothing. Some popular franchise businesses involve fast food restaurants, retail clothing and accessories, home and commercial cleaning services, residential real estate, and personal grooming.

Of course, the first franchise names that come to mind are McDonald's, Burger King, Starbucks, Five Guys, Dairy Queen, Chipotle, KFC, and ServPro Cleaning Services, all of which are very profitable businesses. In addition, there are hundreds of worthy franchise operations that cost less money to enter and generate substantial income.

How a Franchise Works

There are two entities involved in the franchise operation. First is the *franchisor*, the company that owns the brand name, like McDonald's. The other part is the *franchisee,* the person who buys the product name and sells the franchisor's products at an individual store or online. The franchisor provides the location, training, marketing, sales support, advertising, and other requirements needed to operate a business. The company charges the individual store operator a franchise fee to begin the business and takes a percentage of the business revenue.

Purchasing a franchise can cost serious money. For example, McDonald's requires a minimum of $250,000 in cash to be considered for a franchise. You cannot borrow this amount; it must be $250,000 that is unencumbered, and that is just the beginning. Before you are finished, it will cost anywhere from $600,000 to

$1.5 million to purchase a McDonald's franchise. However, other interesting franchise opportunities are available for as little as $10,000.

The following list of popular and successful franchises and their *approximate* buy-in cost, furnished by Franchise Business Review in 2017, will give you an idea of what you can expect to spend to purchase a franchise:

1. Visiting Angels: $77,000
2. MaidPro: $59,000
3. Pinot's Palette: $76,000
4. CertaPro Painters: $135,000
5. Wild Birds Unlimited: $150,000

Do remember that stated costs associated with purchasing a franchise are estimates. Final cost depends on a number of variables, including location.

Franchise Resources for Mid-Career Workers
Here are popular online resources to learn about starting your own business with a franchise. These sources describe the business, furnish franchise costs, provide contact information, and list locations where franchise sites are available. In addition, most provide detailed financial information so that you can determine the company's strengths and weaknesses.

- *Business Franchise Review,* www.franchisebusinessreview. com
- *Entrepreneur,* www.entrepreneur.com. This source is available in magazine format, too. Recent issues contained interesting articles about former corporate workers who started their own businesses with a franchise.
- *Franchise Direct,* www.franchisedirect.com
- *Franchise Opportunities,* www.franchiseopportunities.com
- *Top 100 Franchises,* www.top100franchises.net

Franchise Businesses

Here is a list of franchise businesses to investigate. You may not have heard about all of them, but they are successful and have been in business for decades. Note that many focus on services for the home and commercial building industry, a.k.a. the shelter industry.

1. Pillar to Post Inspection Services
2. Jan-Pro Cleaning
3. Aire Serv HVAC
4. Mr. Appliance Corporation
5. WIN Home Inspection
6. Mr. Electric
7. Jani-King
8. Amerispec Home Inspection Services
9. Matco Tools
10. Anytime Fitness

WHAT KIND OF BUSINESS CAN I START?

The list of business ventures is endless, but a good place to start is with a business whose products and services are in constant need, and in which you have an interest. Food. Shelter. Clothing. Transportation. Technology. Insurance. Education. Healthcare. These are necessities for all regardless of age, gender, geography, race, or religion. Apply the same rules that you did for seeking work in the corporate environment: learn your field of interest, determine your aptitude, define your work experiences, and then translate all into a business venture.

Businesses on Main Street, USA

The next time you leave the house, look at the businesses on either side of Main Street. A majority of them will be stores focusing on food, shelter, clothing, and related products. The point is this: if you want to strike out on your own as an entrepreneur rather than work for someone else, just do it. Play to your passion. Do something that turns you on every day, as Branson said.

Businesses That Do Not Require a Storefront

There are many ways to start your own business that do not require a storefront. The least expensive way to start working on your own is to become an independent sales representative. Independent sales reps usually carry products related to one specific industry. Take cutlery for example. Sales reps working in this narrow market niche might carry products for three or more different manufacturers, both domestic and foreign, and sell them to restaurants both large and small, or to wholesalers that distribute and sell not only knives but also related products such as metal cooking pots and pans. For example, take Mickey, an independent sales representative in New Jersey who sells only cutlery to restaurants in the Mid-Atlantic region. He's been doing that for more than twenty years and has an income exceeding that of a corporate vice president. His marketing slogan? "My products are a cut above the rest."

> **Five Guidelines for Starting Your Own Business**
> 1. Produce and sell the number one life-sustaining product, food, as Colonel Harland Sanders did.
> 2. Provide services for homes and businesses, as Chris and Gary did.
> 3. Sell products of any kind as an independent sales representative, as Mickey did.
> 4. Go to school to earn certification is a field of interest, as Captain King did.
> 5. Follow your passion, as Richard Branson did.

OKAY. WHERE'S THE MONEY?

All entrepreneurs ask, "Where do I find the money to start a business?" It is a valid question. You can start some businesses with little money in your bank account; others require substantial amounts of money. How much money you will need depends on what you intend to do. Let's get practical and explore how you can find the financial resources to start your business:

1. *Your own personal savings.* Some businesses do not cost much to begin operating. If you have only $1,000 saved, it could be enough to get you started. Remember Gary from Philadelphia? How much could it have cost to buy supplies to start a window washing business?

2. *Family money.* Many entrepreneurs borrow start-up money from parents and other family members. Tapping into family money involves trust and confidence. If you are exercising this option, prepare a detailed business plan and present it to your family member just as you would present it to a loan officer at a bank. There is one hard and fast rule about asking family members for money: vow to repay every cent of the loan. You are not a charity case, and family members have their own lives to lead. Present a written statement for family members stating when you will begin repaying the loan and how much each payment will be.

3. *Banks.* Local banks make money by lending money to entrepreneurs. You must create a detailed business plan to attract a banker's attention. There are online sources that give advice about preparing a credible business plan. Approach the most local of banks in your area, an independent bank, not a branch of Wells Fargo or some other multinational banking company. The process is to learn the name of the loan officer and make an appointment for a personal interview to present your business plan, your resume, and career profile. This is a no-nonsense deal, so dress accordingly. Remember that bankers make every effort to minimize risk.

4. *Angel funding sources.* These are individuals or small organizations that provide seed money to entrepreneurs. You can find these sources online, by networking through social media like LinkedIn, or through loan officers at a local bank.

5. *Loans from government organizations.* A variety of government sources provide loans for entrepreneurs. Learn where they are by reviewing the US Small Business Administration website, www.sba.gov.

6. *Venture capital funding.* Large companies that specialize in funding start-up businesses are known as venture capital firms. They generate revenue by lending money to start-up firms that have little downside risk. Usually, they seek businesses that are already generating revenue and that require upwards of one million dollars to expand operations.

MOVING FORWARD

Owning a business requires your undivided attention and much time. However, if you like what you are doing, the time factor becomes insignificant. This oft-repeated advice rings true. *Do what you love, and you will never work a day in your life.* If the risk of starting a business is not your idea of an interesting career path, consider something with more stability, like working in a local, state, or federal government job. In the next chapter, I'll walk you through the process.

CHAPTER TAKEAWAYS

- Plan your work. Work your plan. This is a critical first step when starting your own business.
- Follow your passion when selecting the kind of business you would like to start.
- Select a business that provides basic goods and services for consumers.
- You alone can make a difference by applying your intelligence and energy to an idea about which you are passionate.

PRINT AND DIGITAL RESOURCES

Aluet, Bill. *Disciplined Entrepreneurship: 24 Steps to a Successful Startup.* Wiley, 2013.

Branson, Richard. *Like a Virgin: Secrets They Won't Teach You at Business School.* Virgin Books, 2012.

Branson, Richard. *Losing My Virginity.* Virgin Books, 2013.

Fishman, Stephen. *Working for Yourself: Law & Taxes for Independent Contractors, Freelancers & Consultants.* NOLO, 2011.

International Franchise Expo. www.internationalfranchiseexpo. com. This annual trade show for franchise companies is held each year in New York City and attracts five hundred franchise companies. The franchisor's representatives will give you a detailed description of their businesses and disclose how much money you will need to buy in.

Schiff, Lewis. *Business Brilliant: Surprising Lessons from the Greatest Self-Made Business Icons.* Harper Business, 2013.

Shirk, Martha, and Anna Wadia. *Kitchen Table Entrepreneurs: How Eleven Women Escaped Poverty and Became Their Own Bosses.* Basic Books, 2009.

Tracy, Brian. *GOALS: How to Get Everything You Want, Faster Than You Thought Possible.* Berrett-Koehler, 2010.

Chapter 18

LOCAL, STATE, AND FEDERAL GOVERNMENT JOBS

The American workplace is divided into the public sector and the private sector. The public sector consists of all elected and appointed government jobs at the federal, state, and local levels. The public sector employs workers in jobs as diverse as president of the United States, state senator, governor, city building commissioner, and administrative assistant for the mayor of Waukesha, Wisconsin.

There are approximately 22 million local, state, and federal government jobs according to the Bureau of Labor Statistics. Yes, you read that correctly—*twenty-two million*. Of that number, the federal government alone employs 2.8 million workers. State governments employ 5.1 million. And local governments employ 14.1 million.

LOCAL GOVERNMENT JOBS

Jobs in towns, cities, and counties are just around the corner from every mid-career worker looking for new opportunities. For those who have decided to pursue a career in government or politics, the local level is a good place to start. Here, at the grassroots level, you will learn how government works and the role you can play in it. Former Massachusetts congressman, Tip O'Neill, offered this sage advice for those seeking a career in politics: "All politics is local." All successful politicians must know how it works on their own turf, at the local level.

How do you get started? Begin by reviewing your local government website where you will find a list of both full-time salaried jobs and part-time hourly-pay jobs.

Specific instructions govern application for all government jobs, one of which is applying online. If you see something appealing, complete the application, submit it, and go to the next step, which is making a personal visit to the city offices and asking to see the town manager or mayor personally. If that person is not available, ask to see the administrative assistant. *Do not sit at home and wait for an answer to your online application.*

Proactive Job Hunting for Local Government Jobs

If you do not see a job posting for local government jobs, put on your business attire and with your resume in hand, make a personal visit to the government office and tell the receptionist you are there to see the mayor, or the highest-ranking official for that government entity, about job opportunities. Tell the gatekeeper (the receptionist or administrative assistant) you are there to see the mayor. If you cannot arrange a personal visit with the mayor, or another high-level official, ask the receptionist to give your resume to the mayor or the mayor's administrative assistant. Remember to request a personal interview. Receptionists and administrative assistants have more power than you might suspect in the hiring process. You always want them on your side. Several days later, follow up by calling the mayor or the admin to make sure they have reviewed your resume.

Sometimes government jobs, at any level, are awarded to those who know a prominent government official or businessperson. If you have family members or friends who work in government, use that person as the referral agent. Networking is often a key factor in obtaining a government job.

STATE GOVERNMENT JOBS

Follow the same process to explore jobs at the state level—start by looking up your state government website online. You will find many different departments and a listing of jobs at different locations throughout the state. Follow the instructions for applying online and then visit the office personally, repeating the procedure you used at the local level.

You cannot circumvent the application rules for government jobs because legislation governs the employment process. Always try to use a referral source if you have one.

FEDERAL GOVERNMENT JOBS

The federal government is the country's largest employer and offers a variety of interesting jobs spanning every possible occupation. It employs 2.8 million workers, according to statistics released by the US Office of Personnel Management and the Bureau of Labor Statistics. (Walmart is the second largest employer with 2.3 million workers.)

A common misconception is that federal government jobs are located primarily in Washington, DC. Once again, the BLS statistics set us straight. Eighty-seven percent of federal government jobs are located outside of Washington. There are federal government jobs in every state and in many foreign countries as well.

The processes for finding work with the federal government are sometimes complex and even contradictory. In fact, all federal government departments require that resumes be structured as directed on the job description. Go to the BLS website and read the article titled "How to Get a Job in the Federal Government" by Olivia Crosby. The information and instructions in this article will demystify the federal government employment process, save you time, and possibly lead to the Promised Land of employment.

Note that the federal government does not post its jobs on Internet job boards or advertise them in nongovernment media, and it does not use recruiters. These jobs are posted only on the websites of a federal government department and on the official federal government website, USA Jobs, referenced below.

Government jobs such as senator, representative, or president are not permanent positions. They come and go with periodic elections. However, other jobs exist regardless of the political party in power. They are called civil service jobs, and they keep the wheels of government turning regardless of the party in power. These jobs offer attractive salaries and excellent benefits and are comparable to private sector jobs. For example, a federal government department, such as the Department of Agriculture, hires workers at every level to operate its budget, prepare online and print ads, and conduct informational workshops for agri-businesses, farmers, and the general public. If you are coming from a marketing job in the private sector, your management skills will qualify you for a marketing job in this, or any other, federal government department. The same applies for mid-career workers who have corporate experience in finance. Their skills are transferable and will qualify them for work in places like the Office of Management and Budget, an important department in the executive branch. Expertise you acquired in the private sector will always find a home at one of the many departments operating the federal government.

To learn what positions are available, go to the website of the department that interests you. For example, if you are interested in education-related jobs, go to the website of the US Department of Education, www.ed.gov, and click on "Jobs." When I last checked, I found a position for a lead human resources specialist based in Washington, DC. The salary range was $108,000–$141,000.

Government is something that touches every citizen, and your participation in the process is a significant responsibility. Government jobs, political or civil service, in a country with a population nearing 330 million offer the opportunity to do something meaningful and long-lasting. Yes, one person can make a difference. It is not all partisan politics.

HOW A POLITICIAN CAN MAKE A DIFFERENCE

Elected or appointed political jobs offer opportunities for everyone regardless of education or work history. The most important qualification is passion for completing a mission in your area of interest. Here's an example of how one person followed her passion for improving quality of life for women and children across America as an elected politician. This Colorado representative applied her intelligence, energy, and passion to get the job done. When you read her story, note well what she did for all American workers.

Congresswoman Patricia "Pat" Schroeder

Mrs. Schroeder was a mother of two young children when she decided to make a difference and run for political office in Colorado. She had no family history in politics, no one to pave the way for her through political connections, and no family money to pay for her election campaign. After a hard-fought campaign, she was elected to the United States House of Representatives and went on to serve twelve consecutive two-year terms. Few elected politicians serve for twenty-four years at the federal level.

During her tenure in the House, she became the Dean of Congressional Women, co-chaired the Congressional Caucus on Women's Issues for ten years, served on the House Judiciary Committee, the Post Office and Civil Service Committee, and was the first woman to serve on the House Armed Services Committee. As chair of the House Select Committee on Children, Youth and Families from 1991 to 1993, Mrs. Schroeder guided the Family and Medical Leave Act and the National Institutes of Health Revitalization Act to enactment in 1993, a fitting legislative achievement for her lifetime of work on behalf of women's and family issues. In addition, she was active on many military issues, expediting the National Security Committee's vote to allow women to fly combat missions in 1991.

Another accomplishment was her program to improve the situation of families through passage of the Family Medical Leave Act in 1985. The importance of this Act cannot be understated. The US Department of Labor describes it like this: "The FMLA entitles eligible employees of covered employers to take unpaid, job-protected leave for specified family and medical reasons with continuation of group health insurance coverage under the same terms and conditions as if the employee had not taken leave. Eligible employees are entitled to twelve workweeks of leave in a 12-month period."

When you are in need and the FMLA comes to your support, think of Congresswoman Schroeder. Her story proves that one person can make a difference. If she did it, so can any mid-career worker who chooses to become an elected politician.

RESOURCES FOR EXPLORING FEDERAL GOVERNMENT JOBS

There are many sources of information and support for mid-career workers seeking employment with the federal government. Before you begin your exploration, carefully review all of the sources listed below.

- *USA Jobs,* www.usajobs.gov. This site boasts being the federal government's official job site. It provides general information about working in a federal government job and specific advice about how to begin your search. In addition, this site provides location-specific federal government jobs postings. When I entered my zip code, I found postings for the following jobs right in my backyard:
    - Communications Program Specialist, base annual salary: $125,000.
    - Public Health Veterinarian, base annual salary range: $57,000–90,000.
    - Flight Operations Specialist, base annual salary range: $49,000–64,000.
    - Supervisory Supply Technician, base annual salary: $54,000–70,000.
- *US Office of Personnel Management,* www.opm.gov. Think of this as the human resources department for the federal government. It manages all hiring procedures including recruiting, training, and benefits. In addition, it conducts background checks on all job candidates.
- *The Book of US Government Jobs.* This book, authored by Dennis Damp, is in its 11th edition, which tells you what a valuable resource it is. Over 450,000 copies have been sold. It is available from Amazon, Barnes and Noble, independent bookstores, and the publisher, Bookhaven Press. It has won numerous awards and is the best on the market for understanding how the federal government employment process works. The rules and regulations for government employment can be onerous. This book will help you through the process and save you time.

- *Federal Government Jobs,* www.federaljobs.net. The author of the above-listed book, Dennis Damp, a former federal government employee, operates what is considered the most useful website for current information about federal government jobs. It includes instructions for applying to federal government jobs, government job listings, blogs written by staffing experts, resume writing instructions, and references to additional resources. Make this your first stop for learning about federal government jobs.

MOVING FORWARD

Mid-career workers seeking a new career path frequently overlook government jobs. Do not make that mistake. Jobs at all government levels offer rewarding careers that pay well, provide attractive benefits, provide work satisfaction, and offer attractive pension plans.

Finding work with a large company, a small business, a government agency or starting your own business requires much time and effort. It is a labor-intensive process, and there are times when one needs to call upon outside resources for guidance and support. Where does one find such resources? In the next part, I'll tell you how to access career care providers to lend a hand when you have run out of ideas and are looking for help . . . and a friend.

CHAPTER TAKEAWAYS

- Government jobs pay well and provide attractive benefits.
- Most government jobs are *not* political.
- Applying for government jobs can be challenging. Allow extra time to learn the process.
- Government jobs are not posted on Internet job boards or with recruiters.
- Eighty-five percent of federal government jobs are outside of Washington, DC.
- Elected political jobs offer the opportunity to make a significant difference.

- Using a referral can be an important factor in winning government jobs.
- Prepare a special resume for government jobs following online specifications.

PRINT AND DIGITAL RESOURCES

Damp, Dennis. *The Book of U.S. Government Jobs*. Bookhaven Press, 2011.

Damp, Dennis. *Federal Government Jobs*. www.federaljobs.net.

Part IV

REACHING OUT TO CAREER CARE PROVIDERS

Don't walk behind me. I may not lead.
Don't walk in front of me. I may not follow.
Just walk beside me and be my friend.

—Anonymous,
sometimes attributed to Albert Camus

Chapter 19

CONSULTING WITH CAREER COACHES, CAREER COUNSELORS, AND OUTPLACEMENT SERVICES

There are times when mid-career workers find themselves walking in a dark cloud of anxiety or even depression after being fired or laid off. They look for slivers of daylight but find nothing but more darkness. The universe seems unresponsive. They do not want much, maybe just someone who says, "I understand where you are. Just take my hand and I'll help you out of this mess." That person may be a career coach, career counselor, or an outplacement service, all career care providers.

Reaching out to a career care provider takes courage, understanding, and a good deal of common sense. Where do you find them? What do their services cost? What are their qualifications? And what do these outplacement services really do? All are valid questions. Let's deal with career coaches and counselors first.

CAREER COACHES AND CAREER COUNSELORS

Go online and enter "career coach and career counselor," and you will find an array of hits naming specific individuals, with or without titles. Some are named Joe Smith, Life Coach, or Mary Jones, Executive Career Counselor, or Robert Brown, PhD. Who are the successful ones? Who are the pretenders? Let's look for answers to help you see daylight, to find a break in the dark cloud.

Career coaches are providers who are solution oriented. They focus on helping clients define career objectives, like finding an industry that includes nonprofit companies where passion for the mission is as important as the bottom line. They exude a spirit of optimism, educate you about the job market, and show you how to navigate your way through the world of work. Most will help you craft a resume and provide you with job-hunting rubrics. Some are former human resources directors or executive recruiters. Almost all have experience working in the corporate world.

Career counselors perform many of the same services as career coaches but extend their efforts to uncovering any emotional, behavioral, or psychological barriers that might impede your search for the meaning of work and a new career. Some are certified psychologists or former human resources directors or both. Many hold a master's degree in counseling and are certified by the National Board of Certified Counselors. They can help you work through complex issues, like why it is that you always have problems with authority figures like your former boss.

All career coaches and career counselors charge a fee for their services, which are delivered by phone, Skype, email, or in face-to-face meetings.

Fees for Services

The fees can range from $75 to $500 for a forty-five- or sixty-minute session. Some career coaches and counselors offer package deals that contain a certain number of sessions spread out over a certain amount of time. Others offer their services on an as-needed basis. Personal sessions will cost more than phone sessions. Specialized sessions will cost more than general sessions. For example, some providers work only with executive-level clients, like former presidents, CIOs, CFOs, or CEOs, whose career searches target positions of like kind. Fees for such clients will be considerably higher.

Few coaches and counselors will advertise their fees online, which means that everything is negotiable. Do not hesitate to negotiate a mutually acceptable fee with a provider. Do not be intimidated by a fancy shingle like "Dr. Aldus Geronimo, Certified Career Counselor." Everyone is open to negotiating fees . . . even PhDs.

Career counseling services provided by a certified psychologist or psychiatrist may be covered by your medical insurance. Check with your career care provider and insurance company.

Assessing Provider Credentials

The background and experience of coaches and counselors vary widely. Some have no formal training while others have had training at bricks-and-mortar institutions. Many have completed online certification programs. The most reputable coaches and counselors have written certifications for successfully completing coaching and counseling programs. Here are some of the more reputable training organizations for career coaches and counselors. All award written certifications for successful completion of training courses. Use the information provided by these resources to assess the credentials of career coaches and counselors.

- *International Coach Federation (ICF)*, www. coachfederation.org. This is a highly regarded coaching organization that provides online certification courses for coaches. Access this site for information about the coaching business generally and about suggestions for finding the right coach or counselor that will suit your needs.
- *National Career Development Association*, www.NCDA.org. This respected organization dates back to 1913 and provides not only credentialed programs for coaches, but also assistance for those seeking help in a particular location. For example, go to the website and enter your home zip code in the box beneath the section titled "Need Career Help?" and you will get the names and contact information for coaches and counselors within a fifty-mile radius of your home. Those who successfully complete the NCDA career coaching program receive the Global Career Development Facilitator (GCDF) certificate. When you are interviewing prospective coaches, always ask if they have this certification.

- *Professional Association of Resume Writers and Career Coaches (PARW C/C)*, www.parw.com. This organization provides intensive career coaching training and awards those who successfully complete the course with the Certified Professional Career Coach (CPCC) credential. In addition, PARW C/C offers credentials to coaches who complete training for interviewing techniques and for resume writing, and it offers help for those starting their own businesses.
- *The Academies*, www.theacademies.com. The founder and CEO of this organization is Susan Whitcomb, an author and expert trainer for career coaches. Her work is frequently quoted in the *New York Times* and the *Wall Street Journal*. Coaches who are trained at the Academies are well versed in all facets of career building. Earmark coaches with the Academies certifications.
- *AARP*, www.aarp.org. This organization is no longer focused exclusively on retired workers. For a low membership fee of $16 per year, workers age fifty and over can access their many benefits. One of them is career counseling for unemployed workers or for workers making a career change.

How to Select a Career Coach/Counselor

Select a career coach using the same common-sense rules that you'd apply in making any serious business decision. They are:

1. Make a plan that defines your needs and expectations from a coach or counselor.
2. Contact your network for referrals to professionals specializing in your field of interest and expertise.
3. Go online to find providers in your local area.
4. Interview each person on your list, personally or by phone.
5. Learn the coach's fee structure and how payments are structured.
6. Ask for referrals to their previous or present clients.
7. Ask for a written statement describing their experience in coaching including how many assignments they have completed.

8. Learn their education background, including career coaching certification.
9. Learn if they provide a trial counseling session.
10. Review the extent of their business experience.

Coach Selection Resources

There are online resources that provide information about career coaching generally and about criteria for selecting the right person. Here are three reliable sources.

- *International Coach Federation (ICF),* www.coachfederation. org, is the premier global organization for training life and career coaches. Founded in 1995, the ICF provides professional development and support for its members, in addition to training new coaches seeking certification. The ICF publishes an online magazine titled *Coaching World*. IFC recommends that you ask these questions when interviewing a prospective coach:
  - What is your coaching experience (number of individuals coached, years of experience, types of coaching situations, etc.)?
  - What is your coach-specific training (enrolled in an ICF-accredited training program, other coach-specific training, etc.)?
  - What is your coaching specialty or areas in which you most often work?
  - What types of businesses do you work with most often? And at what levels (executives, upper management, middle management, etc.)?
  - What is your philosophy about coaching?
  - What types of assessments are you certified to deliver?
  - What are some of your coaching success stories (specific examples of individuals who have succeeded as a result of coaching)?
  - Are you a member of ICF? Do you hold an ICF credential?

- *NOOMII, The Professional Coach Directory,* www.
NOOMII.com. This online service recommends coaches
based on your stated goals. NOOMII offers an interesting
approach to recommendations for coaches. After completing
a questionnaire, you are given a number of certified coaches
whose expertise is aligned with your profile and goals. We
suggest that you review their services. We like the cost: *free.*
- *Kathy Caprino, Women's Career Coach and Leadership
Trainer,* http://kathycaprino.com. Kathy is one of the most
celebrated career coaches in the world. She was laid off in
mid-career and after much soul searching started her own
business focusing on career training and coaching. She offers
a free subscription to her weekly newsletter and valuable
rubrics for moving forward in your career. Be sure to read
her article "The Top Five Regrets of Midlife Professionals."
She believes they are:
  ○ I wish I hadn't listened to other people about what I
    should study and pursue.
  ○ I wish I hadn't worked so hard and missed out on so
    much.
  ○ I wish I hadn't let my fears stop me from making change.
  ○ I wish I had learned how to address toxic situations and
    people.
  ○ I wish I hadn't let myself become so trapped around
    money.

Career coaches and counselors are typically caring individuals
who are passionate about lending support and direction to laid-off
or fired workers. Many have had that experience themselves and understand your predicament. When it seems that you are nearing the
end of your own self-help resources, reaching out to a coach or counselor is a wise decision.

WORKING WITH AN OUTPLACEMENT SERVICE
Outplacement is not a mom-and-pop business; rather, it is a large
industry with national or multinational companies in its fold.

Employers frequently provide bricks-and-mortar or virtual outplacement services for mid-level and above workers they let go. This service is expensive and costs the employer upwards of $5,000 per each let-go employee. For high-level executives, outplacement services could cost the employer as much as $25,000 per executive. If your employer did not include outplacement in your severance package, you can purchase it as an individual.

The traditional outplacement service consists of group sessions in an office setting. Weekly or semi-monthly group sessions held at an office location and spearheaded by an experienced leader/teacher, offer much-needed support for laid-off or fired workers. A spirit of mutual support and assistance are invaluable aids to the let-go person still working through the grieving period or in job-hunting mode. It is reassuring to know that you are not alone in this battle. I myself can attest to the effectiveness of this model, having attended group outplacement on-location in Philadelphia after having been laid off from a technology consulting firm that was purchased by a competitor. For example, when I reported to the group leader, he took me into his office for a private counseling session. That was followed by a half-day group meeting with other laid-off workers where we exchanged experiences and offered each other support and direction. Six weekly meetings followed. Our leader provided excellent rubrics for crafting a resume and tips for interviewing. We devoted part of our weekly meetings to reviewing a wide array of companies in the area who were potential employers. Also, we had access to computers and could immediately go to the Internet to access potential employers using the rules we had just learned in class. Most helpful in my experience was the group interaction. I learned that I was not the only one in a tough spot. The entire experience hastened my trip through the grieving process. Try to find an outplacement service that still offers that kind of personal service.

Today some outplacement services are rendered online, by email, phone, Skype, or a combination of these options. Individual attention is what the current model advertises. Services included in most packages are general career counseling, resume preparation, interviewing techniques, industry and company evaluations, cover and follow-up letter writing, and referrals to recruiters or human resources directors. Most outplacement companies advertise one-on-one sessions focused on the items you select.

Outplacement services, particularly in a bricks-and-mortar environment, will be highly beneficial for the newly laid-off worker seeking support, understanding, and direction for moving forward. Finding the service right for you is key. Seek a service that is close to home, provides personal meetings and class meetings, and has a verifiable record of success.

Outplacement Resources

To find an outplacement provider, use the same techniques suggested for finding a career coach. When you go online, make sure to localize your search. If you live in New York, try to find a service in the NY Metro area, not in San Diego. Here are several references to get you started:

- *Reaction Search International,* www.reactionsearch.com. This service ranks outplacement firms located in a specified geographical location, a valuable feature because working with a company close to home renders effective outcomes.
- *Quest Outplacement,* www.questoutplacement.com. Quest offers a variety of one-on-one outplacement packages to individual let-go workers. The cost varies between $850 and $2,950, depending on the length of time and the support items offered. Their support is through phone and online tools. They do not provide an office location.
- *Lee Hecht Harrison,* www.lhh.com. LHH is a multinational recruiting and outplacement firm with three hundred offices scattered throughout the United States and abroad. Home offices are in Woodcliff Lake, New Jersey. The company has been in business for fifty years and has a sterling reputation for quality service.

Always review the reputation of any outplacement firm using the following two sources, which provide references, recommendations, and evaluations that will help you make the right decision:

1. *Glassdoor,* www.glassdoor.com
2. *Outplacing.com,* www.outplacing.com

MOVING FORWARD

Employing a career coach/counselor or an outplacement firm is a serious business decision. Finding the right provider, one with whom you connect personally and professionally, is key to a successful outcome. However, help does not stop here. There are additional services providers that tackle the career rebuilding process from a different perspective. These are faith-based organizations, which are located in every community. To learn more about these additional resources, proceed to the next chapter.

CHAPTER TAKEAWAYS

- Selecting a career care provider is a business decision.
- Always check and verify the credentials of a career care provider.
- Local providers offer the most effective services.
- Craft a plan defining your needs and goals before employing any services.
- Working with a career coach or outplacement firm will keep you focused on your objectives and provide direction to find your way out of the dark cloud of unemployment.

PRINT AND DIGITAL RESOURCES

"8 Tips for Hiring and Using a Career Coach." *Forbes*, September 8, 2014. www.forbes.com/sites/nextavenue/2014/09/08/8-tips-for-hiring-and-using-a-career-coach. Go online and enter "Forbes career coaching" for more information.

Glassdoor. www.glassdoor.com. This site provides free reviews for everything job related, including coaching and outplacement services.

Monster. www.monster.com. Review the article titled "7 Tips for Working with a Career Counselor."

Psychology Today. www.psychologytoday.com. This resource is available as a print or online magazine. It offers a special section titled "Work."

Yates, Julia. *The Career Coaching Handbook.* Routledge, 2014.

Chapter 20

TAPPING INTO FAITH-BASED RESOURCES

Being fired or laid off in mid-career can be one's worst nightmare. Political correctness refers to being let go as a challenge, but a fired or laid-off worker realistically calls it a problem, a *huge problem*, one that needs multiple resources to resolve. When the paycheck stops and you have bills to pay, like a home mortgage or apartment rent, property taxes, car payments, utility bills, insurance premiums, childcare, school or college tuition for the kids, and the unforeseen mega-bill for replacement of a heating system that quits in the middle of the winter, you have more than a "challenge." You have a very serious problem.

Added to the monetary problem is the angst that accompanies being fired or laid off and the tension generated in the job-hunting process. What's left is a worker who needs a comforting hand and down-to-earth friendship in order to move forward and out of the cloud of uncertainty. Finding your way to a new career that offers a paycheck to keep the wolf from the door, plus job satisfaction, plus a sense of purpose, is a multifaceted problem requiring help from multiple sources. Career coaches, counselors, and outplacement services can help fix the multiple problems, but there are other resources as well.

FINDING YOUR WAY OUT OF THE CLOUD
So where does one find support, the kind of support that not only offers practical solutions, but also addresses the various stages of the

grieving process? Many work through it on their own. Others reach out to friends and family. And some workers, who can't find their way out of the cloud on their own or with help from friends, turn to faith-based resources such as:

1. Career workshops offered by a local church or place of worship of any denomination.
2. Discussion groups led by a staff member of the theology department of a college or university.
3. Counseling sessions with members of the clergy.

Each option has merit. Knowing which to use will save time and result in a better outcome. Here's a succinct review of each.

Local Church Counseling Services

Places of worship are noted for providing courses of every kind after Saturday or Sunday services and throughout the week. One does not have to be a member of a particular church to attend, but using the services of your own faith can be reassuring. All are welcome at all churches, at any time.

To learn what is being offered at a local church simply Google its name and look at the website. For example, I entered "Old St. Patrick's Church in Chicago." What I found was an impressive list of services provided by the church staff, including personal counseling from a parish member whose credentials include an MBA from Northwestern and a master's degree in counseling.

Workers living in medium and large cities throughout the country will find a host of career-related services provided by Jewish career services. For example, in Louisville, Kentucky, you will find a very active center, The Jewish Family and Career Services (JFCS). Its services include career counseling, job-hunting advice, and leads for jobs in the local area and nationwide as well.

College and University Spiritual Resources

Some colleges and universities throughout the country have departments of divinity whose reach goes beyond academics. Staff members not only work with students in a traditional academic environment, but also reach out to the community. Outreach includes workshops on traditional theological topics and secular issues such as career planning and counseling for workers seeking support while unemployed.

Everyone who lives within reach of a college or university will find career-related initiatives that come in different flavors. Some are informal discussion groups; others are formal classes held on a regular schedule. For example, one such group is the Princeton Faith and Work Initiative. It meets monthly on a pre-announced Saturday morning at Nassau Presbyterian Church, located on the Princeton New Jersey campus of Princeton University. It is led by Dr. David Miller, who earned his PhD in social ethics from Yale University after working in the private sector for sixteen years in business and finance with multinational companies in the UK and the US. The group describes its mission as follows:

Princeton University Faith and Work Initiative Mission
The purpose of the Princeton Faith and Work Initiative is to generate intellectual frameworks and practical resources for the issues and opportunities surrounding faith and work. The initiative investigates the ways in which the resources of various religious traditions and spiritual identities shape and inform engagement with diverse workplace issues as ethics, values, vocation, meaning, purpose, and how people live out their faith in an increasingly pluralistic world. The initiative explores pressing marketplace topics including ethics, global competition and its ramifications, wealth creation and poverty, diversity and inclusion, conflicting stakeholder interests, and social responsibility.

The group accomplishes its mission through a mixture of teaching, lectures, conferences, discussion groups, and research. Attendees include workers of all rank from companies representing multiple industries.

This is just one example of a spiritual resource from a college that sheds light on the relationship between work and faith, and offers support for workers seeking a new beginning in the workplace. Check online for a college or university near you that offers career-related discussion groups or workshops.

Counseling from a Clergy Member

Advice and guidance are always available from clergy members of your local place of worship. Some clerics will hold one-on-one sessions for general counseling regarding the problems related to your unemployment status. Others will lead group discussions on career-related topics. These are caring, compassionate, and resourceful women and men whose mission is helping people connect faith, work, and family on life's journey.

Some clergy members have broad and deep experience in the secular workplace acquired before they entered the ministry. Many have had teaching and counseling experience. Their networks include hiring managers from companies representing diverse industries. All are sympathetic listeners who offer not only sound advice, but also the hand of friendship to those in need.

MOVING FORWARD

When all else seems to have failed, laid-off workers have another option, seeking help from the God of their faith. The next chapter will shed light on how one can move beyond the temporal for help in the job-hunting process.

CHAPTER TAKEAWAYS

- Spiritual resources offer support, counseling, and friendship.
- If your church has several clergy members, try to connect with those who have had secular workplace experience.
- Some churches offer support from its members who have professional counseling training.

PRINT AND DIGITAL RESOURCES

Christian Counselor Directory. www.christiancounselordirectory. com. Go to this online service to find faith-related services from certified counselors. It provides the names and profiles of counselors throughout the country by zip code.

Christian Jobs. www.christianjobs.org. This is the leading Christian
   job site connecting Christian-friendly employers and job seekers.
   It provides resume help and career coaching as well.

Jewish Family and Career Services. www.jfcslouisville.org. This is
   a very active career center in Louisville, Kentucky. Go online to
   find similar Jewish centers in your own location.

Chapter 21

MOVING BEYOND THE TEMPORAL

Throughout my career in the staffing business, I have witnessed events that have no logical explanation. After applying the rules for solving problems and coming up dry, I believe there must be *something else* working behind the scene that goes beyond the temporal into a realm that includes the supernatural, like a God, a Force, or the Universe.

When seeking help, it is customary to address the care providers, coaches, counselors, ministers, priests, rabbis, by name. But how do you address a deity? What is his or her name? Followers of different faiths call their Gods by different names. The Christians have multiple names for their God depending upon the particular denomination; *Jesus, Father, Savior, Holy One,* are customary. The Jews call their god *Adonai,* which translated means "my Lord." The Muslims refer to their god as *Allah.* The Hindus have multiple gods called by different names like *Krishna, Vishnu,* and *Shiva.* Some believe there is one universal god called the Force. But for our purposes let's call that Supreme Being, God.

Petitioning God when in need is instinctive when all else seems to have failed. You need not be a follower of any particular faith to ask God for help through a tough time, like being fired or laid off. It makes no difference what your religious faith might be. God is God. The name makes no difference.

THERE ARE NO ATHEISTS IN FOXHOLES

So what does all of this have to do with job hunting? You may have heard the proverb "There are no atheists in foxholes." The origin of this proverb is attributed to a World War II correspondent, Ernie Pyle, who reported what was happening on the front line of battle, a very unfriendly place.

For those not familiar with war jargon, here is what it means. When soldiers are on the battlefield and see bombs dropping and bullets flying, and witness their buddies to the left and right being blown to smithereens, these soldiers instinctively call on God to save their lives. Their prayers to God are ones of supplication: "God, please spare my life!"

Job hunting is much like fighting in the trenches, as you may have experienced. Following that traumatic experience, being let go from your job in the middle of a career that you thought was forever, life has not been easy, especially the job-hunting part. You never realized how difficult it is, how competitive it is, how frightening it is when you have bills to pay and nothing seems to be working in your favor. Interviews go wrong, your network seems to have taken an extended vacation, and hiring managers are saying you are overqualified or that they can't afford to pay you market price for your experience and expertise. If you have been fighting on the battlefield of the workplace for six months or more with no success, you will get the analogy. Job hunting is not easy. It is not for the timid. It is not for the faint of heart. The competition is fierce. You never know when and where the next defeat will occur.

The proverb "There are no atheists in foxholes" could easily read, "There are no atheists among job hunters fighting in the workplace for a few bucks to buy food, shelter, and clothing."

GOD AT WORK

My experience as an executive recruiter is replete with examples that point to a Force working with mid-career workers who have made every conceivable effort on their own and with help from career counselors to find solutions to their unemployment challenges. I have named that force working in the background the *Job God*. Here are just a few examples of what I have witnessed.

Sally was a San Francisco resident seeking a step up from her job as a vice president of marketing for a major education publisher. I was conducting a number of searches for which she was eminently well qualified. Sally did not wish to move from San Francisco but was open to relocation for the "right" job. She interviewed for the presidency of a company in Portland, Maine, but it did not work out for a number of reasons. Her next stop was in New York City, where she interviewed for a senior vice presidency with one the country's largest publishers. She liked them and they liked her, but they could not get together on compensation. Her next interview was in Chicago, but the company demands proved impossible for her to meet. Sally, dejected by her job-hunting experiences, returned to San Francisco and tried to determine what happened. Then, unexpectedly, she received a call from the human resources director with a well-known company who invited her to interview for a VP position as head of the newly formed education division. Sally interviewed for the job and got it. Big salary. No relocation. Terrific benefits package. There was no logical reason why this happened. There were candidates who were better qualified for this job, but Sally got it. Why?

And then there was Dick, who lived in San Antonio. He was hired for a marketing position, even though he was the least qualified of five finalists for a position titled "Director of Marketing." There was no logical reason why Dick got that job.

And then we have Jane. Five respectable companies rejected her candidacy claiming she was overqualified. Jane was at the point of depression. Nothing was working for her no matter how hard she tried. Then suddenly she received a job offer from an esteemed employer right in her hometown, one who just a few weeks ago told us, "Sorry, there is nothing available here for Jane."

What was it that led these three job candidates to the Promised Land of employment?

Serendipity? Timing? Fate? These true stories about how Sally, Dick, and Jane found employment working against all the odds went beyond my comprehension. Lacking any evidence for a logical explanation, we hypothesized that it could be something beyond the temporal, something working behind the scene.

SEARCHING FOR TEMPORAL ANSWERS

Others searching for answers might come to different conclusions. If Malcolm Gladwell, author of the bestselling book *Outliers*, had put Sally, Dick, and Jane to the test, he may have found an answer. Gladwell's theory is that if you look hard enough, you will always find an answer to the question "Why did this person succeed?" He even goes so far as to say it could have been the influence of grand-parents, or even *great* grandparents, the culture in which the person lived, date of birth, and a host of other variables. However, none of our three candidates met Gladwell's prime requirement for success: ten thousand hours of experience in a particular field of endeavor, whether it be music, as in the Beatles; or computer technology, as in Bill Gates; or science, as in Albert Einstein.

What accounted for the success of our three candidates? When I found no plausible answers, I hypothesized that it was the *Job God* at work, that Force who controls heaven and earth, the Supreme Being who in some mysterious way is looking out for all of us. Some might say, "Oh my Lord, this is nuts, plain nuts, to posit that God has any interest in how we find work to provide food, shelter, and clothing for our existence here on Earth." Well, everyone has a theory about why things happen as they do, and our theory seems to be as plausible as Gladwell's.

CONNECTING

How do you reach out to your God? What do you say? How do you petition God for a favor such as success in finding a job? You might recall prayers learned in childhood religious training; you memorized them and recited them back to your parents or teacher. They meant little because they did not come from you. Even today, prayers we hear during religious services may sound contrived and hold little meaning. A meaningful prayer must come from you, from your inner core.

So how do you begin the prayer journey? By hastily fabricating one on your smartphone or iPad? By writing it on a sheet of paper in flowery prose? Anything will work, but we suggest composing your prayer in the vernacular of your faith. It does not have to be eloquent or put in writing. Make it conversational. Ask God's help in the same way you would ask one of your friends for a favor. For example, immediately after the attacks on the World Trade Towers on 9/11, two Air Force fighter jets hurriedly took off from their base in Arizona and headed toward New York City and New Jersey to intercept any other attacks. The importance of getting there quickly was more important than fully arming the planes, so they took off semi-prepared. It was a dangerous mission. In a CNN interview with the pilots after the mission was completed, one of them told the interviewer they realized the extreme danger heading into combat without being fully armed, and as they were flying toward the action they prayed the pilot's prayer, "God, don't let me screw this up." A prayer does not have to be eloquent. If you need examples, we offer these resources:

- Tevye's Sabbath Prayer from the play *Fiddler on the Roof*
- The Lord's Prayer, available online or from the Bible
- Sample Prayers. *Thoughts about God.* www.thoughts-about-god.com/reflecting/sample-prayers.htm

A Sample Prayer

If you don't have the time or inclination to access these resources, and if you have not reached out to God since childhood and have no idea about how to begin, try something like this when you need a hand going through one of the steps in the job-hunting process, like the exercise that strikes fear into the hearts of most job seekers, *the interview.*

A Prayer to the Job God

God of all, I'm coming to ask your help. This may not be eloquent, but this is just between You and me, so who cares how it sounds. I'm opening the door to my life and asking you to come in and lend a hand. I need Your help securing employment. I've tried my best, but nothing seems to be working out. I have an interview scheduled with a hiring manager and would appreciate Your support. I'll meet this challenge with a positive attitude and use my intelligence, energy, and passion to get the job done. The bottom line is this, God. When I go in for the interview, I ask that You take my hand and be with me during the entire process. I am sure that with Your help, this will have a favorable outcome. Thanks in advance, God. Amen.

CHAPTER TAKEAWAYS . . . FROM MOTHER THERESA
- Life is an opportunity, benefit from it.
- Life is beauty, admire it.
- Life is a dream, realize it.

PRINT AND DIGITAL RESOURCES

Kushner, Harold S. *When Bad Things Happen to Good People.* Anchor Books, 2004.

Lamott, Anne. *Help, Thanks, Wow!* Riverhead Publishing, 2012.

Payne, Stephen. *The Joy of Work: How to Stay Calm, Confident and Connected in a Chaotic World.* Balboa Press, 2012.

The Prayer Coach. "How to Pray." www.prayercoachingprinciples. wordpress.com/how-to-pray.htm.

Osteen, Joel. *I Declare: 31 Promises to Speak Over Your Life.* Faith Works, 2013.

Warren, Rick. *What Am I Here For?* Zondervan, 2012.

Appendix A

MAJOR CONVENTION CENTERS

E very city and state has convention centers that host trade shows and conferences, which are the best locations to find hiring managers and job opportunities. Managers and directors from sales, marketing, product development, technology, advertising, human resources, event planning, and finance work in the trade show exhibit booths.

What do you do at a trade show? Stop at a booth, introduce yourself, and ask for help securing employment. Does it get any easier than that? Potential employers are not hiding under rocks; rather, they hang out at convention centers, the names and locations of which are just a couple of clicks away.

Go online and contact the convention centers on the list below. Each center will provide the dates and names of the trade shows for the entire year and, in many instances, will provide links to the companies attending. In addition, you will find the price of admission and other pertinent information that will make your visit there more profitable.

MAJOR US CONVENTION CENTERS BY STATE

Alabama
Birmingham-Jefferson Civic Center
www.bjcc.org
2100 Richard Arrington Jr. Blvd. N
Birmingham, AL 35203
(205) 458-8400

Alaska
Anchorage Convention Centers
www.anchorageconventioncenters.com
555 West Fifth Ave.
Anchorage, AK 99501

Juneau Centennial Hall Convention Center
www.juneau.org/centennial
101 Egan Dr.
Juneau, AK 99801
(907) 586-5283

Arizona
Phoenix Convention Center
www.phoenixconventioncenter.com
111 N 3rd St.
Phoenix, AZ 85004-2231
(602) 262-6225

Tucson Convention Center
www.tcc.tucsonaz.gov
260 S. Church St.
Tucson, AZ 85701
(520) 791-4101

Arkansas
Statehouse Convention Center
www.littlerockmeetings.com
#1 Statehouse Plaza
Little Rock, AR 72201
(501) 376-4781
(800) 844-4781

California
Long Beach Convention and Entertainment Center
www.longbeachcc.com
300 Ocean Blvd.
Long Beach, CA 90802
(562) 436-3636

Los Angeles Convention Center
www.lacclink.com
685 South Figueroa St.
Los Angeles, CA 90017
(213) 689-8822

San Diego Convention Center
www.visitsandiego.com
111 West Harbor Dr.
San Diego, CA 92101
(619) 525-5214

Moscone Center
www.moscone.com
747 Howard St.
San Francisco, CA 94103
(415) 974-4000

Colorado
Colorado Convention Center
www.denverconvention.com
700 14th St.
Denver, CO 80202
(303) 228-8000

Connecticut
XL Center (formerly the Hartford Civic Center)
www.xlcenter.com
One Civic Center Plaza
Hartford, CT 06103
(860) 249-6333

Delaware
Delaware does not have a major convention center. Check the convention centers in Baltimore, MD, Philadelphia, PA, Atlantic City, NJ, and Washington, DC.

District of Columbia
Washington Convention Center
www.dcconvention.com
801 Mount Vernon Place, NW
Washington, DC 20001
(202) 249-3000

Florida
Fort Lauderdale/Broward Co. Convention Center
www.ftlauderdalecc.com
1950 Eisenhower Blvd.
Fort Lauderdale, FL 33316
(305) 765-5900

Miami Beach Convention Center
www.miamibeachconvention.com
1901 Convention Center Dr.
Miami Beach, FL 33139
(305) 673-7311

Orange County Convention Center
www.occc.net
9800 International Dr.
Orlando, FL 32819
(407) 345-9800

Tampa Convention Center
www.tampaconventioncenter.com
333 S. Franklin St.
Tampa, FL 33602
(813) 274-8511

Georgia
Georgia World Congress Center
www.gwcc.com
285 Andrew Young International Blvd. NW
Atlanta, GA 30313
(404) 223-4200

Hawaii
Hawaii Convention Center
www.hawaiiconvention.com
1801 Kalakaua Ave.
Honolulu, HI 96815
(808) 943-3500

Idaho
Boise Center
www.boisecenter.com
850 West Front St.
Boise, ID 83702
(208) 336-8900

Illinois
McCormick Place
www.mccormickplace.com
2301 S. Lake Shore Dr.
Chicago, IL 60616
(312) 791-7000

Navy Pier
www.navypier.com
600 East Grand Ave.

Chicago, IL 60611
(312) 595-PIER

Indiana
Indiana Convention Center
www.icclos.com
100 South Capital Ave.
Indianapolis, IN 46225
(317) 262-3400

Iowa
Iowa Events Center
www.iowaeventscenter.com
730 Third St.
Des Moines, IA 50309
(515) 564-8000

Kentucky
Kentucky International Convention Center
www.kyconvention.org
221 Fourth St.
Louisville, KY 40202
(502) 595-4381

Louisiana
Ernest N. Morial Convention Center
www.mccno.com
900 Convention Center Blvd.
New Orleans, LA 70130
(504) 582-3023

Maine
Cumberland Convention Center
www.theciviccenter.com
One Civic Center Sq.
Portland, ME 04101
(207) 775-3481

Maryland
Baltimore Convention Center
www.bccenter.org
1 West Pratt St.
Baltimore, MD 21201
(410) 649-7000

Massachusetts
Boston Convention and Exhibition Center
www.bostonconventioncenter.com
415 Summer St.
Boston, MA
(617) 867-8286

John B. Hynes Convention Center
www.massconvention.com
900 Boylston St.
Boston, MA 02115
(617) 867-8286

Michigan
Cobo Conference/Exhibition Center
www.cobocenter.com
One Washington Blvd.
Detroit, MI 48226
(313) 877-8777

Minnesota
Mayo Civic Center
www.mayociviccenter.com
30 Civic Center Dr. SE
Rochester, MN 55904
(507) 281-6184

Duluth Entertainment Convention Center
www.decc.org
350 Harbor Dr.
Duluth, MN 55802
(218) 722-5573

Minneapolis Convention Center
www.minneapolisconventioncenter.com
1301 Second Ave. S
Minneapolis, MN 55403
(612) 335-6000

Mississippi
Mississippi Coast Convention Center
www.mscoastconventioncenter.com
2350 Beach Blvd.
Biloxi, MS 39531
(228) 594-3700

Missouri
Kansas City Convention
www.kcconvention.com
Convention & Entertainment Centers
301 West 13th St.
Suite 100
Kansas City, MO 64105
(816) 513-5071

America's Center
www.explorestlouis.com
701 Convention Plaza
St. Louis, MO 63105
(800) 325-7962

Montana
Butte Silver Bow Civic Center
www.butteciviccenter.com
1340 Harrison Ave.
Butte, MT 59701
(406) 497-6400

Mansfield Convention Center
www.greatfalls.net/mansfieldcenter.com
4 Park Dr.
Great Falls, MT 59401
(406) 455-8510

Helena Civic Center
www.helenaciviccenter.com
340 Neill Ave
Helena, MT 59601
(406) 461-8785

Nebraska
CenturyLink Center
www.centurylinkcenteromaha.com
455 N. 10th St.
Omaha, NE 68102
(402) 341-1500

Nevada
Las Vegas Convention and Visitors Authority
www.lvcva.com
3150 Paradise Rd.
Las Vegas, NV 89109
(702) 386-7100

New Hampshire
Check the convention centers in Maine and Massachusetts.

New Jersey
Atlantic City Convention Center
www.accenter.com
2301 Boardwalk
Atlantic City, NJ 08401
(800) 214-0663

Meadowlands Exposition Center
www.mecexpo.com
355 Plaza Dr.
Secaucus, NJ 07094
201-330-1172

Edison Convention Center
www.njexpocenter.com/eb&cc
97 Sunfield Ave.
Edison, NJ 08837
(732) 661-1205

Garden State Convention & Exhibit Center
www.gsec.com
50 Atrium Dr.
Somerset, NJ 08873
(732) 417-1400

Wildwoods Convention Center
www.wildwoodsnj.com/cc
4501 Boardwalk
Wildwood, NJ
(609) 729-9000

New Mexico
Albuquerque Convention Center
www.albuquerquecc.com
Second & Tijeras NW
Albuquerque, NM 87102
(505) 842-9918

New York
Buffalo Niagara Convention Center
www.buffaloconvention.com
Convention Center Plaza
Buffalo, NY 14202
(716) 855-5555

Jacob K. Javits Convention Center
www.javitscenter.com
655 West 34th St.
New York, NY 10001
(212) 216-2000

North Carolina
Charlotte Convention Center
www.charlotteconventionctr.com
100 Paul Buck Blvd.
Charlotte, NC 28217
(704) 339-6000

Metrolina Expo Center
www.metrolinatradeshowexpo.com
7100 Statesville Rd.
Charlotte, NC 28221
(704) 596-4650

North Dakota
Check the convention centers in Minnesota and South Dakota.

Ohio
Duke Energy Convention Center
www.duke-energycenter.com
525 Elm St.
Cincinnati, OH 45202
(513) 419-7300

Cleveland Convention Center
www.clevcc.com
500 Lakeside Ave.
Cleveland, OH 44114
(216) 928-1600

I-X Center
www.ixcenter.com
6200 Riverside Dr.
Cleveland, OH 44135
(216) 676-6000

Dayton Convention Center
www.daytonconventioncenter.com
22 E. Fifth St.
Dayton, OH 45402
(937) 333-4700

Seagate Convention Centre
www.toledo-seagate.com
401 Jefferson Ave.
Toledo, OH 43604
(419) 321-5007

Oklahoma
Cox Convention Center
www.coxconventioncenter.com
1 Myriad Gardens
Oklahoma City, OK 73102-9219
(405) 602-8500

Cox Business Center
www.coxcentertulsa.com
100 Civic Center
Tulsa, OK 74103
(918) 894-4350

Oregon
Oregon Convention Center
www.oregoncc.com
777 N Martin Luther King Blvd.
Portland, OR 97232
(503) 235-7575

Pennsylvania
Pennsylvania Convention Center
www.paconvention.com
1101 Arch St.
Philadelphia, PA 19107
(215) 418-4700

Lawrence Convention Center
www.pittsburghcc.com
1000 Ft. Duquesne Blvd.
Pittsburgh, PA 15222
(412) 565-6000

Rhode Island
Rhode Island Convention Center
www.riconvention.com
One Sabin St.
Providence, RI 02903-1814
(401) 458-6000

South Carolina
Charleston Convention Center
www.charlestonconventioncenter.com
5001 Coliseum Dr. North
Charleston, SC 29418
(843) 529-5050

Palmetto International Exposition Center
www.palmettoexpo.com
One Exposition Ave.
Greenville, SC 29607
(864) 233-2562

South Dakota
Sioux Empire Fairgrounds
www.souixempirefair.org
Sioux Empire Fair Office
4000 W 12th St.
Sioux Falls, SD 57107
(605) 367-7178

Tennessee
Nashville Convention Center
www.nashvilleconventionctr.com
601 Commerce St.
Nashville, TN 37203
(615) 742-2002

Texas
Austin Convention Center
www.austinconventioncenter.com
500 E. First St.
Austin, TX 78701
(512) 404-4000

Kay Baily Hutchinson Convention Center
www.dallasconventioncenter.com
650 S. Griffin St.
Dallas, TX 75202
(214) 939-2750

George R. Brown Convention Center
www.houstonconventioncenter.com
1001 Avenida de las Americas
Houston, TX 77010
(713) 853-8090

Henry B. Gonzalez Convention Center
www.sahbgcc.com
200 E. Market St.
San Antonio, TX 78205
(877) 504-8895

Waco Convention Center
www.wacocc.com
100 Washington Ave.
Waco, TX 76702
(254) 750-5810

Utah
Salt Palace Convention Center
www.saltpalace.com
100 SW Temple
Salt Lake City, UT 84101
(801) 534-4777

Dixie Convention Center
www.dixiecenter.com
1835 Convention Center Dr.
St. George, UT 84790
(435) 628-7003

Vermont
Check the convention centers in Massachusetts and New York.

Virginia
The Greater Richmond Convention Center
www.richmondcenter.com
403 N. Third St.
Richmond, VA 23219
(804) 783-7300

The Virginia Beach Convention Center
www.vbcvb.com
1000 19th St.
Virginia Beach, VA 23451
(757) 385-2000

Washington
Meydenbauer Center
www.meydenbauer.com
11100 NE Sixth St.
Bellevue, WA 98004
(425) 637-1020

Washington State Convention & Trade Center
www.wscc.com
800 Convention Place
Seattle, WA 98101-2350
(206) 694-5000

Spokane Center
www.spokanecenter.com
334 W. Spokane Falls Blvd.
Spokane, WA 99201
(509) 353-6500

West Virginia
Charleston Civic Center
www.charlestonciviccenter.com
200 Civic Center Dr.
Charleston, WV 25301
(304) 345-1500

Wisconsin
Wisconsin Center
www.wisconsincenter.org
Wisconsin Center District
400 W. Wisconsin Ave.
Milwaukee, WI 53203
(414) 908-6000

Wyoming
Casper Events Center
www.caspereventscenter.com
One Events Dr.
Caspar, WY 82601
307-235-8441

Appendix B

CONVENTION CENTER AND TRADE SHOW SPOTLIGHT

A number of state convention centers and trade shows deserve special attention because of their strategic locations and the important conferences they attract. Having attended hundreds of trade shows across the country, I know the top sites and trade shows and would like to share some of them with you. Here are my recommendations.

California
The Moscone Center, www.moscone.com. Located in the heart of San Francisco, the Moscone Center hosts some of our largest conventions. In recent years, it attracted the National Auto Dealers Association, the Molecular Medicine Convention, and a number of "Green" conferences dealing with environmental products and services.

Florida
The Orange County Convention Center, www.occc.net. Located in Orlando, this is one of busiest convention centers in the world, hosting national and international conferences. There are two separate facilities a block apart, and each can accommodate tens of thousands of visitors at one time. The convention halls are massive, so be prepared to do a lot of walking. Some conventions to attend here are the Orlando Home Show, the Florida Educational Technology Conference, and the Golf Industry Show. The Golf Show attracts 500 companies, which means there are 500 potential employers all

gathered under one roof. Attendance usually runs over 50,000. Do you like the sporting industry? Attend the Golf Show.

The Tampa Convention Center, www.tampaconventioncenter.com. This is one of the premier conference centers in the Southeast. It accommodates medium-sized conferences that attract hundreds of companies exhibiting their products and services. Its location is on the waterfront in downtown Tampa.

Miami Beach Convention Center, www.miamibeachconvention. com. The Americas' largest jewelry show meets here each year. It is sponsored by the Jewelers International Showcase (JIS) and features three shows annually that attract thousands of exhibitors and thousands of attendees. A recent show had approximately 1,200 exhibit booths. The JIS trade shows attract companies and attendees from 50 countries in the Caribbean, Latin America, and North America. If you like gold, silver, diamonds, rubies, and pearls, this is the place to go to find a job in the jewelry industry.

Georgia

The Atlanta Convention Center, www.atlconventioncenter.com. This large conference facility (more than 800,000 square feet) attracts many national and international trade shows each year. For example, the International Society for Technology in Education (ISTE) recently held a convention here that attracted 15,000 attendees. This conference hosted 500 exhibiting companies that produce educational technology products for K-12 and higher education. More than 4,500 company representatives worked the booths.

Hawaii

The Hawaii Convention Center, www.meethawaii.com. This one-million-square-foot convention center is just down the street from famed Waikiki beach and is one of the best of its kind in the world. It holds many large and small conferences around the calendar, many of them with exhibitors staffed by key employees, like hiring managers. Check out the careers, listed under "jobs," on their website.

Ready for some sun, surf, and a luau on weekends after convention hours? That's working in Hawaii. Does it get any better than that?

Illinois

McCormick Place, www.McCormickplace.com. This facility, located on the shore of Lake Michigan in Chicago, is Illinois's largest convention facility. Go there now on your smartphone, iPad, tablet, or laptop. Click on "full calendar" and then go to the "monthly calendar." This convention center is one of the most popular in the country because of its central location. Some of the shows it hosts annually are the Progressive Insurance Boat Show, the International Home and Housewares Show, and the National Restaurant Show.

Go to the website and click on the show title, and it will take you to that particular website. You will find all the information you need including the names and addresses of hundreds of companies that will be exhibiting.

Indiana

The Indianapolis Convention Center, www.icclos.com. This popular conference center hosts many national and regional conferences representing all industries. Its central location and reasonable attendance fees make it a popular location. One of the most important regional conferences held here is the Indiana Bankers Association. I checked out a recent conference and it listed all of the attending banks, many of which were national financial institutions. And *it listed the names of the attendees from each bank.* Pay dirt!

Iowa

Iowa Events Center, www.iowaeventscenter.com. The Iowa-Nebraska Equipment Dealers Association hosts the Iowa Power Farming trade show here each year. The convention brings together under one roof manufacturers and dealers of farming equipment, all of which are potential job targets. If you are interested in agribusiness, where better to find a job than in Iowa, at the Iowa Events Center in Des Moines?

When I reviewed the Iowa Events Center website, I found an interesting array of job opportunities in marketing, sales, events management, and food and beverage operations.

New York

The Javits Convention Center, www.javitscenter.com. This is one of the best-known convention centers in the world and attracts an impressive array of important conventions. Companies that exhibit here always send their executives and hiring managers, making the Javits one of the best venues for job hunting.

One of the most interesting and important annual conventions held at the Javits each October is Photo Plus Expo. It attracts approximately 300 companies that exhibit their latest products and services for the photography and imaging industry. Hundreds of hiring managers staff the various exhibit booths. Attending this conference is not only a good job-hunting experience, but also an interesting learning experience.

Washington, DC

The Washington Convention Center, www.dcconvention.com. Our nation's capital has one of the most frequently used convention centers for regional and national trade shows and exhibits. Check the website frequently because conventions in Washington draw a large number of both vendors and attendees. Hiring managers and top-level executives of major companies attend DC conventions.

In addition, many large DC hotels, such as Marriott, Holiday Inn, and Hilton, host trade shows, and I suggest checking their websites for conference information. If you cannot find it online, call the hotel and ask to speak with the conference manager.

BEST TRADE SHOWS FOR JOB HUNTING BY INDUSTRY

The following list of annual trade shows by industry could be your ticket to finding a new career path after being fired or laid off. Click on the show nearest to your location or the show focusing on an area of interest, like photography, housing, food, shelter, travel, or educational technology and publishing. The organizations listed below hold conferences in different locations each year.

To get you started, I'm focusing on only seven industries: Education, Insurance, Healthcare Transportation, and the *Big Three*, Food, Shelter, and Clothing.

Education

The Education Industry is truly worker friendly. Many work in this industry because find a sense of mission, job satisfaction, and attractive compensation. At all of these exhibits, you will meet hiring managers working for companies like College Board, Educational Testing Service (ETS), Scholastic, McGraw-Hill, Texas Instruments, and Pearson. Here are some of the best.

American Booksellers Association (ABA), www.bookweb.com. The ABA holds an annual conference and several regional conferences where you can see many companies in the print and digital publishing industry. The 2016 show was held in Chicago and the 2017 annual convention (BookExpo) at the Javits Center in New York. This is the largest publishing conference in the United States.

American Association of School Administrators (AASA), www.aasa.org. Hundreds of companies exhibit here to display their products to school superintendents and other high-level school administrators. The companies attending this convention are publishers and producers of instructional materials, school supply companies, bus companies, insurance companies, security companies, and more.

Association of Educational Publishers, www.aepweb.org. This organization sponsors an annual conference in June each year in Washington, DC. Attendees include high-level educational technology and publishing company executives, all of whom are hiring authorities. In 2013, this organization merged with the Association of American Publishers (AAP), www.publishers.org.

American Library Association (ALA), www.ALA.org. This conference focuses on books and digital products related to public and school libraries and online education. It is a fascinating show with hundreds of exhibitors from the education, publishing, and online learning industries. When you are on this website, click on "Education and Careers" for job opportunities with the organization.

Association for Supervision and Curriculum Development (ASCD), www.ascd.org. Members of ASCD are involved with curriculum matters at K-12 schools. Thousands of these administrators, called curriculum coordinators or assistant superintendents for instruction, attend this show.

American Society for Training and Development (ASTD), www. astd.org. This nonprofit organization focuses on training and professional development for educators and government workers. It holds an annual conference in a major city, plus four regional conferences throughout the country. A recent conference met in Dallas and attracted approximately 9,000 attendees from 80 different countries. More than 300 companies exhibited their products and services. The fee for entrance to the exhibits? Free! Track the annual and regional conferences because this is where you will meet many employers in the flesh, each one being the source for employment.

International Literacy Association (ILA), www.literacyworldwide. org. This organization is for teachers and administrators who teach reading and literacy to K-12 students. When you access this site, click on "career center," where you will find ten or more pages of open positions for entry-level and experienced workers. If you have any experience in education, and are interested in literacy education, this is the conference to attend to explore job opportunities.

International Society for Technology in Education (ISTE), www. iste.org. This show focuses on products and services related to educational technology and meets each June at a different location. If you are interested in an industry that makes a difference for kids, this one is for you. Do not miss it, because here you will find hundreds of exhibitors under one roof. Each is a potential employer.

In addition, there are a number of curriculum-related education conferences held annually in different locations. They are:

National Association of Biology Teachers (NABT), www.nabt.org
National Council for the Social Studies (NCSS), www.ncss.org
National Council for Teachers of English (NCTE), www.ncte.org
National Council of Teachers of Mathematics (NCTM), www.
nctm.org
National Science Teachers Association (NSTA), www.nsta.org
Software and Information Industry Association (SIIA), www.siia.
org
Texas Computer Education Association (TCEA), www.tcea.org

International Education Book Fairs
There are several international publishing conventions each year and if you are in the area, plan to attend. Companies from America and other countries host exhibits staffed by workers who will tell you about job opportunities *and* provide the names and contact information for hiring managers. Foreign companies may be looking for workers to represent their interests in America and you might be the one for such a job. Here are some of the best international trade fairs in the education and communication industries.

Frankfurt Book Fair, www.buchmesse.de/en/company. This convention attracts 7,000 exhibitors from around the world and is the mother of all international book fairs. It meets in Frankfurt, Germany, every October. Can you imagine 7,000 potential employers under one roof?

The London Book Fair (LBF), www.londonbookfair.co.uk. This major bookseller event meets in London each spring. It attracts close to 1,000 exhibitors ranging from retail booksellers to educational publishers and communications companies in general.

Bologna Children's Book Fair, www.bolognachildrensbookfair. com. This interesting book fair focuses on products related to K-12 education. Hundreds of companies publishing books and digital products exhibit here. Bologna, Italy, is the host city for this annual conference. Check it out if you happen to be in Italy in spring.

Beijing International Book Fair (BIBF), www.combinedbook.com. If you find yourself in China during the month of August, visit this fascinating conference to meet more than 500 exhibitors from around the world, with an emphasis on Asian companies. This is a long way to go to meet American companies, but you will find many of them exhibiting alongside their foreign counterparts. Beijing is the host city for this annual conference.

Insurance

Like it or not, you need insurance. Many insurance companies have been in business continuously for more than a hundred years and are attractive places for long-term employment. The industry hosts many conventions throughout the calendar year in many different cities. Here is one on the largest conferences in the industry.

The National Association of Mutual Insurance Companies (NAMIC), www.namic.org. This is one of the largest insurance professional organizations in the business, and it hosts an annual convention at a different location each year. Recent conferences were held at the Gaylord National Resort and Conference Center in National Harbor, Maryland, and at the San Diego Convention center. It is hard to beat the insurance industry for long-term employment. The best place for information about insurance trade shows is the *Insurance Journal.* Visit the website at www.insurancejournal.com.

Healthcare

Under the broadly defined label of "healthcare," there are numerous subgroups: pharmaceuticals, physicians, radiologists, certified nurse midwives, medical equipment producers, physical therapists, medicinal packaging, and the like. There is no large catch-all healthcare convention, but there are many small conventions serving segments of the healthcare industry. Many of these conventions are local or regional in scope. Here are some of the larger national conventions sponsored by professional healthcare organizations.

- *Nurse Practioners in Women's Healthcare, NPWH,* www. npwh.org
- *Federation of International Medical Equipment Suppliers,* www.fimeshow.com
- *Radiographical Society of North America,* www.rsna.org
- *Healthcare Information and Management Systems Society,* www.himss.org
- *American Society of Clinical Oncology,* www.asco.org
- *International Society for Pharmaceutical Engineering (ISPE)* sponsors the annual Pharma Expo conference. www. pharmaexpo.com
- *American College of Nurse-Midwives,* www.acnm.org
- *American Physical Therapy Association,* www.apta.org

The largest in this group is Pharma Expo, www.pharmaexpo. com, a convention devoted to packaging medicines and medical equipment. A recent convention was held in Denver in conjunction with PACK EXPO, the national convention for the general packaging industry. Approximately 1,800 exhibitors and over 30,000 industry workers attended this convention.

Transportation

In addition to food, shelter, and clothing, transportation is one of the basics for modern living. The transportation industry conducts hundreds of conventions each year in locations throughout the country and it would be impossible to list all of them. Google "auto shows," add the largest city close to home, and you will find all the information you need. Here is an example of a major transportation show to get you started:

New York International Auto Show, www.autoshowny.com. This conference is one of the largest auto shows in the country and hosts hundreds of companies, which exhibit on the floor of the Javits Center. Attend this conference, and you will find potential job opportunities in the automobile industry. Guaranteed.

Food

This huge industry includes everything imaginable including fast foods, beverages, restaurants, online grocery shopping, and hospitality. There are many local, regional, and national conventions catering to the food industry. Check out those listed below.

Specialty Food Association, www.specialtyfood.com. This show attracts over 1,200 exhibitors and tens of thousands of attendees. Its location changes each year.

The International Restaurant and Food Service Show, www.internationalrestaurantny.com. Meet 500 exhibiting companies and 16,000 workers in this interesting venue at the Javits Center in New York. The convention is the best in this market niche.

National Restaurant Association, www.show.restaurant.org. How can you beat a convention with 2,000 exhibitors (all potential employers) and 45,000 attendees? If your interest is the restaurant niche, plan to attend this conference, which meets at McCormick Place in Chicago each year. For general information about this part of the food industry, contact the National Restaurant Association, www.restaurant.org.

Clothing

This industry includes a number of specialties, like children's clothing, sportswear, women's fashion apparel, textile manufacturing, footwear, and exercise gear, just to name a few. As a result, there are no national conventions catering to the clothing industry as a whole. The best way to find trade shows in a specialty of the clothing industry is to conduct an online search for your area of interest.

One of the best and largest shows for women's accessories is held at the Javits Center in New York each January and is known as Apparel Sourcing USA. Check it out at www.10times.com/apparelsourcing.

Shelter

You might recall that one of the three necessities for survival is shelter. Therefore, it is not surprising there are many home and commercial building shows throughout the United States that attract thousands of companies exhibiting their products. Each one is a potential employer. Where do you find them? At conference centers throughout the country. For example, do you live in or near the Chicago area? There are several home shows in different area locations hosting many hundreds of exhibitors. Go to www.chicagohomeshow.net to find out more.

There are so many home shows that it would take many pages to list all of them here. An easy route to find these conferences is to Google "home trade shows" in your local area. Sometimes these shows combine home building and improvement companies with garden and horticulture organizations. As an example of what you will find, I'll highlight just two:

National Association of Home Builders (NAHB), www.hahb.com. The annual convention is called the NAHB International Builders Show. At this show, you will find approximately 1,000 exhibiting companies, all potential employers. If the shelter part of survival intrigues you, attend this show and other home shows that take place in major cities. In addition to providing an opportunity to meet hiring managers, or workers who can lead you to them, this show will provide an education about how the *shelter* industry works in the US. Attend this show or other regional home shows, and your knowledge of the housing industry will increase exponentially.

Philadelphia Home Show, www.phillyhomeshow.com. This conference takes place in Philly each February and hosts hundreds of exhibitors. Most are local companies, but some are national, too. While you are there, remember to have one of those famous Philadelphia cheesesteak sandwiches. Also, visit the Philadelphia Art Museum where you can have your picture taken beside the famous bronze of Rocky. And remember to save a day to visit Independence Hall and the Liberty Bell.

One of the most important takeaways in this book it to build conference attendance into your work plan. A trade show at a major convention center is a unique opportunity to meet hiring managers, in the flesh, to build a relationship which will ultimately lead to a job.

ALSO BY JOHN HENRY WEISS

Welcome to the Real World: A Complete Guide to Job Hunting for the Recent College Grad

Operation Job Search: A Guide for Military Veterans Transitioning to Civilian Careers

You may leave comments for the author at Weiss4Jobs@aol.com.

ACKNOWLEDGMENTS

My thanks to the many workers who contributed to *Moving Forward*. They reviewed the manuscript, in whole or in part, and offered encouragement and valuable advice for making improvements.

Laura Bair. Digital designer and wedding consultant.

Marilyn Baker. Certified nurse midwife and staff midwife with Robert Wood Johnson Hospital Hamilton . . . and my wife.

Vicki Smith Bigham. Pre-K–adult education teacher, administrator, trainer, and industry consultant.

Lisa Bingen. Director of marketing, Heinemann Publishing Company.

Diana Cano. Executive director of Enterprise Technology Strategy, Innovation and Architecture, based in Princeton, NJ.

Eric Gootkind. Certified senior professional in human resources (SPHR); director of employment and employee relations, Measured Progress, Inc.

Olga Greco and Caroline Russomanno. Editors, Skyhorse Publishing Inc., who were responsible for making this book a reality. Thank you Olga and Caroline!

Tina Hamilton. Educational technology consultant and contractor.

John C. Meeker, PhD. Author, encore career coach, executive recruiter, teacher.

Ed Meell. Founder of MMS Education, former editorial director for McGraw-Hill films, US Army Veteran.

Alice Miller. Station manager/program director, WWFM, The Classical Network.

Joanne Silvestri. Education account director, Salesforce.com.

Vincent Vezza. Author, senior vice president, teacher.

Chris Weiss. Video producer, founder, and partner, RaffertyWeiss Media.

INDEX